The Real Sterling Crisis

The Real Sterling Crisis

Why the UK needs a policy to keep
the exchange rate down

Roger Bootle and John Mills

CIVITAS

First Published September 2016

© Civitas 2016
55 Tufton Street
London SW1P 3QL

email: books@civitas.org.uk

ISBN 978-1-906837-83-9

Independence: Civitas: Institute for the Study of Civil Society is a registered educational charity (No. 1085494) and a company limited by guarantee (No. 04023541). Civitas is financed from a variety of private sources to avoid over-reliance on any single or small group of donors.

All publications are independently refereed. All the Institute's publications seek to further its objective of promoting the advancement of learning. The views expressed are those of the authors, not of the Institute, as is responsibility for data and content.

Designed and typeset by
lukejefford.com

Printed in Great Britain by
4edge Limited, Essex

Contents

Authors

One of the City of London's best-known economists, **Roger Bootle** is Chairman of Capital Economics, one of the world's largest independent economics consultancies, which he founded in 1999. Roger is also a Specialist Adviser to the House of Commons Treasury Committee, an Honorary Fellow of the Institute of Actuaries and a Fellow of the Society of Business Economists. He was formerly Group Chief Economist of HSBC and, under the previous Conservative government, he was appointed one of the Chancellor's panel of Independent Economic Advisers, the so-called 'Wise Men'. He was a visiting Professor at Manchester Business School from 1995 to 2003, and between 1999 and 2011 served as Economic Adviser to Deloitte. In July 2012, it was announced that Roger and a team from Capital Economics had won the Wolfson Prize, the second biggest prize in Economics after the Nobel.

Roger Bootle studied at Oxford University, at Merton and Nuffield Colleges, and then became a Lecturer in Economics at St Anne's College, Oxford. Most of his subsequent career has been spent in the City of London.

Roger has written many articles and several books on monetary economics. His latest book, *The Trouble with Europe*, examines how the EU needs to be reformed and what could take its place if it fails to change. This book follows *The Trouble with Markets* and *Money for Nothing*, which were widely acclaimed. His earlier book, *The Death of Inflation*, published in 1996, became a best-seller and was subsequently translated into nine languages. Initially dismissed as extreme, *The Death of Inflation* is now widely recognised as prophetic. Roger is also joint author of the book *Theory of Money*, and author of *Index-Linked Gilts*.

Roger appears frequently on television and radio and is also a regular columnist for *The Daily Telegraph*. In The Comment Awards 2012 he was named Economics Commentator of the year.

John Mills is an entrepreneur and economist with a life-long political background in the Labour Party, leading him to being its largest individual donor. He graduated in Philosophy, Politics and Economics from Merton College, Oxford, in 1961. He is currently Chairman of John Mills Limited (JML), a consumer goods company specialising in selling products requiring audio-visual promotion at the point of sale, based in the UK but with sales throughout the world. He was a member of Camden Council, specialising in housing and finance, almost continuously from 1971 to 2006, with a break during the late 1980s when he was Deputy Chairman of the London Docklands Development Corporation. He was a parliamentary candidate twice in 1974 and for the European Parliament in 1979.

John has been Secretary of the Labour Euro-Safeguards Campaign since 1975 and the Labour Economic Policy Group since 1985. He has also been a committee member of the Economic Research Council since 1997 and is now its Vice-Chairman. During the period running up to the June 2016 referendum he was Chair of The People's Pledge, Co-Chairman of Business for Britain, Chair of Labour for a Referendum, Chair and then Vice-Chair of Vote Leave and Chair of Labour Leave, which became independent of Vote Leave two months before the referendum.

John is the author of numerous pamphlets and articles and he is a frequent commentator on radio and television. He is Chair of the Pound Campaign which produces regular bulletins advocating that economic policy should be far more focused on the exchange rate than it has been for many decades, arguing that an over-valued pound has been largely responsible for UK deindustrialisation and our grossly unbalanced economy. He is the author or joint-author of nine books, these being: *Growth and Welfare: A New Policy for Britain* (Martin Robertson and Barnes and Noble, 1972); *Monetarism or Prosperity* (with Bryan Gould and Shaun Stewart; Macmillan 1982); *Tackling Britain's False Economy* (Macmillan 1997); *Europe's Economic Dilemma* (Macmillan 1998); *America's Soluble Promises* (Macmillan 1999); *Managing the World Economy* (Palgrave Macmillan 2000); *A Critical History of Economics* (Palgrave Macmillan 2002 and Beijing Commercial Press 2006); *Exchange Rate Alignments* (Palgrave Macmillan, 2012) and *Call to Action* (with Bryan Gould; Ebury Publishing 2015).

Authors'
Acknowledgements

This pamphlet is the result of a collaboration between two people of both similar persuasions and opposite ones. John Mills has been a life-long committed supporter of the Labour Party. Indeed, in recent years, he has been Labour's largest individual donor. By contrast, although Roger Bootle has no formal political allegiance, his sympathies are generally with the Right.

Yet both individuals are an unusual combination of economist and entrepreneur. John Mills founded and runs JML, the consumer products group. Roger Bootle founded and runs Capital Economics, the economics research house. Interestingly, both of us read Philosophy, Politics and Economics at the same institution – Merton College, Oxford.

And both of us are very worried about the shape of the British economy and the role of an excessively strong exchange rate in distorting it and holding back its growth rate. Both of us want to see the exchange rate occupying a key role in the setting of UK economic policy.

We gratefully acknowledge the help of staff at Capital Economics, especially Paul Hollingsworth, in obtaining data and preparing charts. Also, we are extremely grateful to Professor John Black, and to participants at a seminar we held in London in March 2016 to discuss an early draft of the work. As usual, none of the above is at all responsible for any errors of commission or omission. These remain our responsibility. Furthermore, the views expounded here are those of the authors writing in their personal capacities. The individuals and companies referred to above, both named and unnamed, are not necessarily in agreement with them.

Civitas's Acknowledgements

Civitas is very grateful to the Nigel Vinson Charitable Trust for its generous support of this project.

Executive Summary

- Many people in the market and much of the commentariat are currently concerned with the recent weakness of the pound on the exchanges. They are barking up the wrong tree. The real sterling crisis is that the pound has been too high.

- Accordingly, the Brexit-inspired bout of sterling weakness was extremely good news for the British economy.

- Far from panicking about the lower pound, the UK authorities should be concerning themselves with the question of how they can ensure that the pound continues to trade at a competitive level in the future.

- The exchange rate of the pound is vital to the success and health of the UK economy and the fact that it has long been stuck at much too high a level bears much of the responsibility for the economy's current ills.

- These results have not exactly been intended. Despite the exchange rate's importance for the UK, for almost 25 years there has been no policy for it. As a policy variable the pound has been left in a state of neglect, in the belief that other things (principally inflation) should determine policy, and/or because 'the markets know best'. This latter belief mirrors the establishment's faith in the financial markets prior to the crisis of 2008/9.

- But we have subsequently learned, if we did not know it beforehand, that, left to their own devices, the financial markets may systematically misprice financial variables, and that they may behave in a reckless way in the pursuit of individual short-term gain that puts the long-term stability of the financial system at risk.

- Interestingly, although such reasoning is now widely accepted in relation to the equity and property markets, recently no one seems to have made these points about foreign exchange markets – until now.

- This would be surprising to an earlier generation of economists schooled in the crises and policy disputes of the 1930s. They were brought up to believe that, not only could markets malfunction dramatically, but they could produce and sustain a destabilising set of exchange rates, which could have devastating consequences for the real economy.

- No one was more aware of the importance of exchange rates than John Maynard Keynes. In the 1930s, a series of devaluations and the imposition of protectionist trade policies were major contributors to the Great Depression. Following that experience, Keynes was determined to establish for the post-war world a global exchange rate regime that placed equal obligations on deficit and surplus countries to adjust, thereby ensuring that the new system did not have a deflationary bias.

- This is most definitely not the system that we have today. Rather, financial pressures to adjust are felt by deficit countries, while surplus countries, such as China, Germany, the Netherlands and Switzerland, feel very little pressure at all. The result is a deflationary tendency for the world as a whole – felt particularly strongly within the eurozone.

- The UK is not part of this deflationary tendency – although we suffer from its consequences. And we do suffer acutely from exchange rate misalignment. There has been a deep-seated tendency for sterling to settle at too high a level for the health of the UK economy.

- This is for two main reasons. First, because of the UK's political stability and the extraordinary liquidity and attractions of its asset markets, it has a decided tendency to attract private capital flows that push up the real exchange rate.

- Second, because of a history of inherently strong domestic inflationary pressure, the UK policy authorities have tended to welcome, and even encourage, a strong exchange rate as a way of bearing down on UK inflation.

- The results are devastating. On the financial side, persistent current account deficits undermine the country's financial future. The UK is now a substantial net debtor. Excessive borrowing would be bad enough but the UK has increasingly sold real assets. The result is that not only is the present borrowing from the future, but there is also a loss of national control over important parts of the economy.

- This weak external position particularly affects our manufacturing sector, bolstering the forces making for its decline as a share of GDP.

- This then diminishes our prospective rate of productivity growth (since productivity growth is stronger in manufacturing than services), intensifies the problems associated with employing lower-skilled workers, increases inequality, and accentuates the regional divide.

- Accordingly, an economic policy that accorded a much greater role for the exchange rate would potentially bring significant benefits.

- As things stand, however, we do not have a free hand in adopting an exchange rate policy. The G7 specifically forbids the deliberate manipulation of exchange rates to gain competitive advantage.

- Mind you, this has not stopped Japan and the eurozone following closet policies of exchange rate depreciation. Outside the G7, China and Switzerland, among umpteen others, have put the management of the exchange rate centre-stage. By contrast, as so often, the UK authorities are left playing 'goody two shoes'.

- There are ways in which the UK could adhere to its formal G7 commitments while effectively pursuing a policy that puts the maintenance of a competitive exchange rate centre-stage. These include putting less reliance on a policy of high interest rates. Continued fiscal stringency plus use of the Bank of England's Prudential Policy toolkit offers a way of doing this. In addition, measures could be taken to make UK real assets less attractive to foreigners.

- Of course, we recognise that competitive devaluation is a zero sum game. Any attempt by the UK to gain competitiveness through a lower exchange rate could be nullified if other countries followed suit. In practice, in current conditions, when the UK is now only a medium-sized player in the world economy, direct retaliation on any scale is not likely.

- Moreover, the UK has been a loser from other countries' depreciations – including by the eurozone. It would not be a case of the UK trying to boost its economy by following a mercantilist prescription in order to increase its exports. The key point is that the UK is running a very large current account deficit.

- A change of policy regime to give greater weight to the exchange rate would necessarily involve some changes to the current inflation targeting regime. But that need not constitute a barrier. Inflation targets are not the last word in macroeconomic policy and plenty of other countries do not allow their policy to be completely dominated by inflation concerns. But it should be possible to fashion a policy regime which retains inflation targets while giving significant weight to the exchange rate.

- Ideally, the world should move towards a new international policy regime that puts exchange rates centre stage and seeks to maintain exchange rates at a reasonable level in relation to the economic fundamentals. But the UK cannot wait for this to happen.

- With the British people having voted to leave the EU, this is an ideal time for the British government to pursue an alternative policy framework. Indeed, setting a policy that would establish and maintain a competitive exchange rate for sterling is the single most important thing that a government can do for the promotion of a prosperous Britain.

Part One

The Problem

1

The impending economic disaster and the pound's role in causing it

Unless something changes, the UK economy is heading for the rocks. This is not because of the consequences of Brexit. On the contrary, the factors that we identify in this pamphlet that cause us such unease predate Brexit, or even the chance of it, and have practically nothing to do with it.

On the face of it, the British economy does not look too bad. But we are not paying our way in the world. Every year, we are borrowing and selling assets to the tune of about 5% of GDP. This is rapidly increasing the amount of our economy that is owned by foreigners.

This would not matter so much if we were using the money provided by foreigners to invest in productive capacity. But we are not. UK investment is extremely low. We are borrowing and selling assets in order to maintain our standard of consumption.

If things continue as at present then in 10 years' time we will have transferred to foreigners assets and ownership of assets amounting to 50% of one year's GDP. With this transfer goes a stream of income, paid to foreigners, out of what we produce in the UK. This will mean that for any given level of what we produce here in the UK (GDP), less will be available to be enjoyed by UK citizens. And if, as at present, foreign wealth holders buy UK real assets, along with the financial transfer goes a substantial amount of control over our economy.

At a time of low interest rates, as at present, the cost of being a net debtor is relatively low. But eventually, of course, interest rates will rise. At that point the cost of the UK being a net debtor would be much higher than at present. Accordingly, the UK could be storing up a problem for the future much larger than it currently imagines.

This outturn would be bad enough if the alternative were to squeeze our living standards now in order to protect and preserve our financial position and the level of our living standards in future. But this is not the situation. Our failure to pay our way derives from the weakness of net exports. Our economy is still operating a substantial way below full capacity. In that case, it should be possible to increase net exports and boost GDP. In other words, the thing that is hurting our living standards in future, is also reducing our incomes today.

If we were able to increase our net exports this would not only boost incomes and employment but it would do so in parts of the economy that have recently done relatively badly – the parts that have been heavily dependent upon manufacturing, thereby helping to address some of our country's problems with inequality.

Moreover, there are links between the current account deficit and the UK's other serious deficit, namely the fiscal one. The financial balance of the UK private sector, UK public sector and the overseas sector must sum to zero. Accordingly, if the government tries to improve its financial position (i.e. the gap between expenditure and tax revenue) without there being an improvement in

Britain's overseas balance, then this can only happen through a worsening of the private sector financial balance, which is often difficult to achieve. Another way of putting this is that policies of austerity often fail.

By contrast, a spontaneous improvement in the current account of the balance of payments would usually improve the financial balance of both the public and private sectors. Higher incomes (from net exports) would automatically improve the financial balance of the private sector and, as they pay taxes on this income (and receive fewer state benefits because of increased income) the public deficit will fall.

The role of the exchange rate

There is more than one reason for our country's weak position on the balance of its overseas income and expenditure (the current account of the balance of payments). Moreover, there is a plethora of problems in the British economy that are not directly connected with the weakness of our balance of payments and cannot be addressed by changes in the value of the currency. Real lasting economic success, and successful dealings with other countries, depend upon building real competitive advantages that are difficult to replicate.

Nevertheless, these real factors are difficult to change in the short term. Moreover, sometimes the exchange rate can be stuck at the wrong level and this can be a source of severe difficulty, even if the 'real' sources of competitive advantage are set favourably.

It is our contention in this paper that too high a level of the pound on the foreign exchanges – the exchange rate against other currencies – is a leading cause of the UK's large current account deficit and that this has major adverse consequences for our economy. Quite simply, for countries heavily engaged in international trade, as the UK is, the exchange rate is the most important price in the economy. Too high a level of the pound will tend to restrict our exports (by making them more expensive) and stimulate imports (by making them cheaper).

Moreover, the exchange rate has a critical bearing on another crucial variable – the profit rate. Other things equal, a higher exchange rate reduces profits and boosts real wages and the real value of other sources of consumer income. Reduced profits tend to lead to lower investment – and lower investment leads to weaker growth and hence lower living standards in future.

But the squeeze on profits is not uniform across the economy. On the contrary, it will be felt by industries engaged in exporting and/or competing with imports. We refer to exports of goods and services, goods and services that would be exported, imports of goods and services, and goods and services that could be imported, as tradables.

A high exchange rate diminishes the price of tradables relative to non-tradables, and thereby diminishes the profit rate of industries producing tradables relative to those producing non-tradables. Furthermore, an exchange rate that undergoes substantial fluctuations will cause substantial fluctuations in the profit rate in industries that produce tradables. This variability will diminish the attractions of investment in tradable industries.

Accordingly, an exchange rate that is too high for extended periods will tend to lead to an unbalanced economy – with too small a manufacturing sector. It is our contention that this is exactly what has happened in the UK.

It is often argued that the UK's problems with its external trade – and hence with its manufacturing industry – originate with real factors, such as the rise of China, that have little, if anything, to do with the exchange rate. Such views are partly justified, and partly dangerous nonsense. The UK steel industry has recently faced an existential crisis which is widely blamed on the cheapness of steel production in the emerging markets, especially China. In fact, in 2014 the UK imported more than four times as much steel from the EU as from the whole of Asia. The exchange rate is seriously relevant to this.

What is the right value for the pound?

By how much is the pound over-valued? Or is it, post-Brexit, now at the right level? There is no hard and fast answer, but we can begin to make some suggestions about orders of magnitude. First, we can track movements in the real effective exchange rate, that is to say, the pound's average value, once account is taken of movements in costs and prices in different countries.

When trying to gauge how over– or under-valued a currency is, it is important not to be fixated upon the exchange rate against one particular currency. The most likely candidate for such currency fixation is the dollar. Yet the UK does much more of its trade with countries that don't use the dollar, with the eurozone being the most important. Accordingly, the best way to measure the value of the pound is to take the average of its value against the currencies used in British trade, with the weight of each currency in the basket governed by the weight of that currency in Britain's overall trade. The measure that does this is the trade-weighted index of the pound, sometimes known as the effective index of the pound.

Yet it is important not to be fixated by the nominal value of this index. A country's price competitiveness is governed by the relationship between the value of its currency and the level of domestic costs and prices compared to costs and prices abroad. For instance, if a country undergoes a 10% fall in its currency but also experiences a 10% rise in its costs and prices relative to those abroad, then its price competitiveness will not have changed. Accordingly, to measure changes in price competitiveness economists usually focus on the *real* exchange rate, that is to say the nominal rate adjusted for changes in relative costs and prices across countries.

Even when these two adjustments are made, judging by how much a currency may be over-valued is more of an art than a science. But we can have a stab at coming to an answer. As Figure 1 shows, the last time that the UK ran a tolerably low current account deficit was in the period immediately after the pound's ejection from the ERM in September 1992. This provides a guide to what should be a competitive exchange rate for the UK.

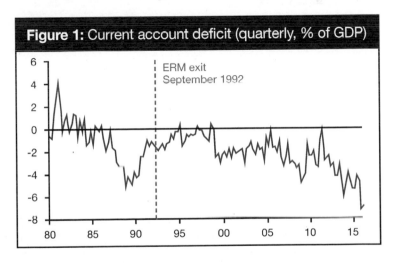

Figure 1: Current account deficit (quarterly, % of GDP)

It suggests that on the Bank of England's measure of the pound's average value, the so-called effective exchange rate, the pound should probably be somewhere close to 75-80, compared to 100 in 2005.

But as Figure 2 shows, starting just before the election of the Labour government in 1997, and continuing afterwards, the pound rose sharply. There followed a 10-year period of rough stability - but stability at too high a level. Indeed, during this period the pound was at roughly the same level that it had been at prior to it being forced out of the ERM in September 1992. (The history of the real exchange rate over this period is very close to the nominal rate.)

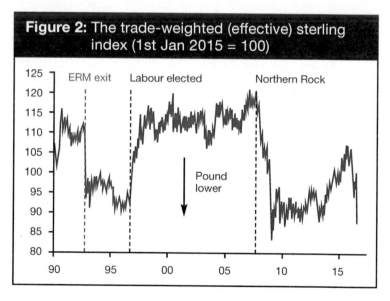

Figure 2: The trade-weighted (effective) sterling index (1st Jan 2015 = 100)

Its value took a dramatic dive immediately after the financial crisis in 2008/9, which returned its value roughly to where it had been in the immediate wake of the ERM crisis – and at one brief point even lower.

After that, however, the effective exchange rate of the pound rose. At its recent peak in November 2015, it stood 30% above the trough reached in March 2009. After the Brexit-inspired drop, in early July, the exchange rate stood roughly where it was after the ERM exit, and slightly above the trough that it reached after the financial crisis in 2009. Something like this may be the right level for the UK to rebalance its economy.

We can also draw on the evidence of direct price comparisons. To make a more general assessment of whether prices are high or low in the UK it is useful to compare prices to those in several other countries. Figure 3 shows comparative price levels for various OECD countries. These data are for May 2016.

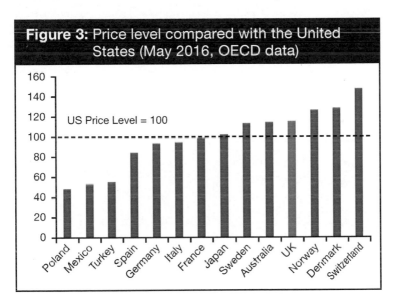

Figure 3: Price level compared with the United States (May 2016, OECD data)

This chart fits with conventional wisdom. For example, it shows that prices in the UK are generally much *higher* than in much poorer economies such as Poland, Mexico and Turkey. It also shows that prices in the UK are much *lower* than in Switzerland, Denmark and Norway.

Less obviously, Figure 3 suggests that in May the general price level was higher in the UK than in most other advanced economies. For example, it was 15% higher in the UK than in the US; 16% higher than in France; 13% higher than in Japan; and 24% higher than in Germany. At face value, this suggests that the pound was over-valued. The fall of the pound after the Brexit vote will have altered these figures considerably.

After the Brexit-inspired fall of the pound, it was trading at a competitive level that hadn't been experienced for many years. We believe that this will prove to be an extremely good thing for the UK economy.

But can the pound be kept somewhere near this competitive level? That is a question that we address in the later part of this pamphlet. First, though, we need to discuss in more detail quite where we are – and how we got there.

2

The current position of overseas trade and net wealth and where we are heading

Recently the UK has been running a very large current account deficit – around £90bn per annum, or 5% of our GDP – matched by borrowing and sales of capital assets to finance the shortfall of overseas revenue over expenditure. How has such a large deficit come about? Is this sustainable? How can such a large deficit be good for the economy? What consequences does it have? If we want to reduce the deficit, or even turn it into a surplus, what policies are there available to the UK authorities to enable them to achieve this? These are the questions that this pamphlet tries to answer. But before we do so we must first tackle a niggling issue of measurement.

Are the balance of payments figures reliable?

The short answer is 'no'. All macro-economic data are unreliable but the data on overseas payments may be particularly so. And this is especially true when economies pass through rapid structural change, as the UK has done over the last 30 years.

Indeed, we know that if you aggregate all the current account positions in the world you find that the world as a whole is in deficit. Yet until we start to trade with Mars (or some other planet) this cannot be. Clearly there is a significant measurement problem.

The balance of payments figures must balance – that is to say, if there is an excess of imports over exports the money to pay for this needs to be found from somewhere. We can sell assets or borrow money. In an ideal world there would be reliable statistics available on all parts of the balance of payments. Unfortunately, we do not live in such a world. The truth has to be pieced together from incomplete data.

Suppose that there are exports or sources of overseas income that the statisticians don't record. For any given reported imbalance of trade in goods, if recorded income from services (or property income) does not match this deficit then it must be presumed that some sort of capital inflow has provided the finance (or the government's foreign exchange reserves have been run down).

The UK is particularly prone to such under-recording since its service sector is so big and it is heavily involved in international capital markets. This means that the UK's current account deficit is probably overstated by the official data, and the balance of payments data are prone to frequent, and sometimes substantial, revision. Figure 4 shows the current estimate for the current account deficit relative to estimates made over the previous two years. In some periods, the revisions have been quite substantial, although this doesn't alter the overall picture.

Indeed, it is unlikely that mismeasurement can occur on a scale sufficient to eradicate the deficit, or even substantially to reduce it. The recent trend in the deficit has been profoundly adverse, as shown in Figure 5. To explain this deterioration, the various distortions that we know about would have to have been getting

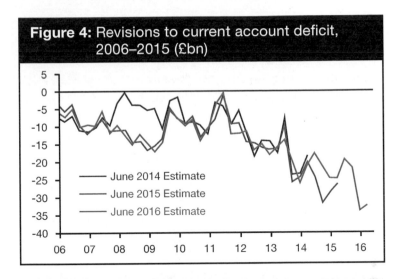

Figure 4: Revisions to current account deficit, 2006–2015 (£bn)

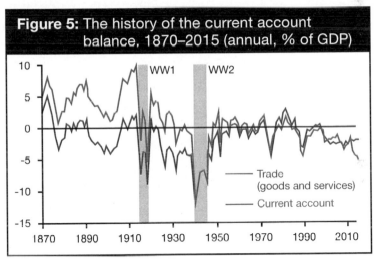

Figure 5: The history of the current account balance, 1870–2015 (annual, % of GDP)

worse. And, as this pamphlet establishes, it is not as though the deterioration in the UK's current account position is without explanation. We know full well why it has deteriorated. We do not need an alternative explanation founded on mismeasurement. The poor performance of Britain's overseas trade is part of a wider pattern of disappointing performance.

An overall economic perspective

That said, the performance of the UK economy since the 2008 financial crash has not been bad compared with many other western countries, although it has been much worse than some parts of the world, particularly around the Pacific Rim. We have much to be thankful for and, when criticising our record, some reasonable perspective is therefore required.

There may be deficiencies in the way our economy is structured and it may in a number of important respects be out of balance, but its absolute performance still compares reasonably well with much of the rest of the world. Ranked in order of size, measured at market exchange rates, the UK economy comes in at number five or six, behind only the USA, China, Japan, Germany and sometimes France.

In terms of gross domestic product (GDP) per head on a purchasing power parity basis, however, our performance has clearly slipped. As measured by the International Monetary Fund (IMF) we come in at 29 out of 188 countries, 29 out of 188 according to the World Bank and 40 out of 230 measured by the US Central Intelligence Agency (CIA). The UK therefore has a very substantial economy with average living standards which are higher than in many other parts of the world, but we have lost our historic pre-eminence and many other countries have already overtaken us, while others are threatening to do so as our growth rate lags behind theirs.

The UK's relative prosperity is partly the result of the fact that the Industrial Revolution started here and we have therefore been increasing our output per head over a long period of time – much longer than in many other parts of the world. During the 19th century, the UK had a higher level of GDP per head than almost anywhere else, although the USA was catching up fast. Clearly we have slipped back some considerable distance from this enviable position since then.

The crucial issue for the future is whether this tendency for us to lose ground in relation to other countries is going to continue and whether our relatively low rate of growth, which is responsible, is likely to be maintained.

Predicting future economic outcomes is always fraught with problems, because there are so many variables. But there are several key reasons for worrying that, even after post-Brexit anxiety has run its course, and even without anything unexpected going wrong, the UK economy may grow slowly over the coming few years.

Weak investment

The first major UK economic weakness is that the proportion of our GDP which we invest rather than consume every year is desperately low. In 2015, excluding Research and Development, it was 13%. Some context for realising just how low this percentage is given by the fact that the world average, measured on a comparable basis, was 25.3% and for China it was 47.8%.

Admittedly, China's investment share in GDP is abnormally high. Not only is much of this investment wasted but the excessive rate of investment threatens to cause a sharp drop in GDP growth – or even a recession – if it adjusts sharply. The Chinese authorities face the difficult task of reducing the share of investment in GDP and increasing the share of consumption.

But, putting China aside, the UK's investment share is low compared to most industrialised countries. As with many other issues in economics, there are considerable measurement difficulties associated with investment spending. Considerable amounts of spending on intangibles, including software development and branding, may achieve significant commercial advantage for individual firms – and real income gains for the economy as a whole – yet may be misclassified in the national accounts.

Because of the structure of the UK economy it is possible that the UK has a disproportionately large share of such spending. Accordingly, appropriately measured, the UK's investment rate is probably not as low as the official figures imply. Nevertheless, it is highly unlikely that measurement issues can explain more than a small fraction of the UK's recorded investment deficiency.

There is worse news, however, in the detail. Of the UK investment total in 2014, only 21% was spent on the type of investment – manufacturing broadly defined – which is most likely to increase productivity. Of the remainder, 17% was spent by the public sector on roads, schools, housing, etc., all of which may be highly desirable on social grounds but which do little directly to increase output per head and hence the growth rate in the short-term. Of the other remaining 62%, just over half was spent on private sector housing construction and the remainder on building commercial premises and service sector activities such as opening new restaurants, none of which, again, contribute significantly to productivity increases.

Thirteen per cent is a very low investment percentage, but when depreciation – running in 2013 at 11.4%

of GDP – is deducted from it, only about 1.5% is left. Faced with these figures, it is not difficult to see why productivity in the UK is virtually static. Furthermore, 1.5% of GDP is not even sufficient to keep up the value of our accumulated capital assets in relation to our rising population, which is currently increasing by at least 500,000 people a year – about 200,000 from indigenous growth and 300,000 from immigration.

If you divide the total accumulated capital assets of the UK – worth £8.5trn at the end of 2014 according to the Office for National Statistics (ONS) – by the total population of the UK, which was then 64.6m – you reach a figure of about £130,000. To avoid diluting down our accumulated capital, we therefore need to spend at least 500,000 x £130,000 – i.e. £65bn – every year just to avoid slipping backwards. Clearly, we are a very long way from doing this. With no net investment per head of the population taking place at all, unless we benefit substantially from some other favourable extraneous factor, it is not realistic to think that we are going to see output per head going up to any significant extent.

Manufacturing squeezed

The second major problem with the UK economy is that we have allowed our manufacturing sector to decline to an extremely low level. As late as 1970, almost a third of our GDP came from manufacturing. The share is now barely 10%.

The absence of good quality manufacturing jobs has contributed strongly to the increases in both regional and socio-economic inequality which have been such a pronounced development in recent decades. Moreover, if manufacturing is the strongest source of productivity increases, the smaller the proportion of GDP that it comprises then, other things equal, the lower the rate of productivity increase in the economy as a whole.

Manufacturing plays a key role in our foreign trade. Despite our small manufacturing sector, about 55% of all our export earnings are from goods rather than services, and although we have a substantial foreign trade surplus on services, this is more than offset by a much bigger deficit on goods – £88bn compared to £126bn in 2015. As a result, we have not had a trade surplus since 1982 or an overall current account surplus since 1985.

The UK's problem – reflected across much of the western world – is that internationally tradable low- and medium-tech manufacturing has been largely wiped out by competition from Asia, leaving us dependent on high-tech exports – aerospace, aircraft engines, pharmaceuticals, motor vehicles and arms sales. Over and above this, in many key markets, the UK has lost out to other developed countries.

There is a view that we need not worry about manufacturing's decline. We should simply accept it and rely on services, where we have a strong comparative advantage. We disagree with this view.

The problem is that the sectors in which we excel, important though they are, do not produce enough to fill the gap between our overseas income and our overseas expenditure. Moreover, they, in turn, are also eventually going to be vulnerable to competition from lower cost countries.

And we are at risk of other pitfalls. Can we be confident, for instance, that the City of London will retain its pre-eminent position? And what would we do if its earnings fell back significantly?

We don't think we can or should lay down what proportion of the economy should be accounted for by manufacturing. That is for the market to decide – once the exchange rate is roughly at the right level. But, given the importance of manufacturing in international trade, and given the plunge in the UK's share of manufacturing in GDP, and the price sensitivity of manufacturing output, we would be surprised if a substantial improvement in the UK's trade balance could be achieved without it being accompanied by a significant rise in manufacturing's share in GDP.

The current account

Our weak trade balance is a major contributor to the poor state of our overall current account position. The table below sets the scene.

Table 1: UK balance of payments breakdown, £bn				
Year	Trade balance	Net investment income from abroad	Net transfers abroad	Total
2008	-46.4	5.3	-14.1	-55.0
2009	34.7	5.4	-15.8	-44.8
2010	43.0	20.2	-20.7	-43.1
2011	-26.2	19.6	-21.7	-29.1
2012	-33.9	-2.2	-21.9	-61.4
2013	-34.2	-10.3	-26.9	-76.4
2014	-34.4	-23.8	-25.0	-85.0
2015	-36.7	-37.0	-24.7	-100.3

Source: ONS BNBP Balance of Payments Quarterly Releases

While our trade deficit, although substantial, is reasonably stable, our net income from abroad has recently seen a very sharp deterioration. From being nearly £20bn in surplus as recently as 2011, it was a negative £37bn in 2015 – a massive negative swing of £57bn.

There is inevitably some volatility in these figures, and there may well be some improvement in them over the coming years. But a significant part of this deterioration is itself a product of the UK running large current account deficits over many years. Such deficits worsen the UK's net asset position and, other things equal, this will lead to a weaker investment income balance. This, in turn, leads to an even weaker net asset position. There is, therefore, an underlying highly adverse trend to our net income from abroad which is likely to produce major problems for us in future. (A higher exchange rate also has the effect of worsening the investment income balance as it diminishes the sterling value of income earned abroad, while leaving the sterling value of income earned by foreigners in the UK unchanged. See later.)

The speed of this deterioration has probably been increased by the way that our deficits have been financed. Whereas in the past it was normal for the UK to attract fixed interest capital (which was held in bank deposits and/or bonds), while the UK typically invested abroad in real assets and/or equities, which tended to have a higher rate of return, in recent decades the UK has taken in a higher proportion of direct investment and equity capital, thereby worsening the relationship between the income earned on foreign assets and the income paid out on foreign assets held in the UK.

Net transfers abroad are also on a rising trend. The largest component is our net contribution to the European Union, which ran at £11bn in 2015. After Brexit this should fall back sharply – hopefully to zero. The remainder is split roughly evenly between net remittances abroad, which are likely to go up if migration to the UK continues at its current very high level, and foreign aid programmes, to which all our major parties are committed. The net result of all these trends is that the UK's overall balance of payments deficit exhibits a strongly rising trend. In the first quarter of 2016 it reached 6.9% of GDP. For 2015 as a whole, the deficit was 5.4% of GDP. In percentage terms this was easily the highest deficit in the whole of the developed world.

Trade not the problem?

Given that the main culprit for the recent deterioration in the overall current account balance is the deterioration in net investment income, while the trade deficit has been broadly stable, there is an argument that exchange rate policy, which is designed to affect the trade balance, is otiose. It is to the change in investment income that we need to direct attention.

But this argument is misguided on five counts:

(i)   The surprising thing is not that the investment income balance has deteriorated recently but rather that it held up so well for so long. This may well be explained by the risky nature of many of the UK's international assets. In any case, although we can hope that it will improve, we cannot take this for granted. We need to take the current level of the investment balance as it is.

(ii) As it happens, a lower exchange value for sterling would improve the net balance of investment income.

(iii) While the size of the trade deficit at about 2% of GDP is much smaller than the overall current account (about 5%), nevertheless, it is still a deficit. Why is it deemed OK for the UK to be running a trade deficit of 'only' 2%, when Germany runs a huge surplus?

(iv) If the UK is to run at a high level of domestic demand and to use up all available spare capacity, the trade deficit would be higher.

(v) Much of the wider adverse economic impact of the current account deficit, including the effects on UK manufacturing, the regional divide and inequality, stem from the trade deficit.

From creditor to debtor nation

The effect of these large and chronic deficits has been to turn the UK from a net creditor to a significant net debtor. ONS figures do not show a consistent pattern year to year but between decades there has been a very marked change. Whereas in the 1980s the UK always had assets exceeding liabilities, during the 2000s liabilities exceeded assets by about £82bn throughout the decade. By 2015 this figure had risen to almost £270bn.

These figures highlight another major concern about the UK economy which is the volume of debt which it now sustains, not least that part of it owed by the government. Clearly, the government deficit needs to be reduced to much more manageable proportions. The key issue is whether this can be done if the country continues to have a foreign payments deficit as large as the one currently being experienced.

It is a fallacy of composition to believe that what might be the obviously sensible way for an individual whose expenditure was greater than his or her income to bring the two back into balance - by cutting expenditure or increasing income - would work in the same way for the economy as a whole. What an individual does has negligible impact on the whole economy, but what the government does – because of the scale of its expenditure - is very different. The crucial fact is that if the household and corporate sectors are very roughly in balance – i.e. neither net borrowers nor net lenders on a very major scale – the government deficit has to be more or less the same size as the foreign payments deficit. That is roughly the position shown in Table 2. Unless the private sector financial balance can be squeezed, for the government deficit to be reduced, the overseas deficit has to fall also – and vice versa.

If the government pursues austerity to try to reduce its deficit then to the extent that it succeeds, this may well reduce the current account deficit but the channel through which this would happen is by reduced aggregate demand cutting back the demand for imports.

Equally, a spontaneous improvement in the financial position of the private sector – perhaps through reduced consumption or investment – would lower the current account deficit but again by reducing aggregate demand and cutting back on demand for imports. But this would hardly count as an advance! Quite apart from causing a waste of economic potential, it would worsen the government's deficit.

What is needed to improve both the current account balance and the government's financial position

Table 2: UK net lending (+) and net borrowing (-) by sector, £bn

Year	Public sector	Non-financial Corporations	Financial Corporations	Households	Foreign Balance	Net Totals
2000	11.8	-0.8	-56.6	22.7	22.8	0.0
2001	4.1	-4.1	-53.5	31.8	21.7	0.0
2002	-23.4	21.0	-41.7	20.1	24.1	0.0
2003	-40.6	38.1	-24.5	6.4	20.6	0.0
2004	-45.1	46.5	-17.5	-6.9	22.9	0.0
2005	-47.0	47.2	-7.3	-10.4	17.6	0.0
2006	-41.0	36.6	-12.6	-16.9	33.9	0.0
2007	-44.2	29.5	-10.9	-12.1	37.7	0.0
2008	-76.8	40.8	-5.8	-12.9	54.8	0.0
2009	-160.5	59.5	6.0	50.6	44.4	0.0
2010	-150.4	59.5	-23.2	71.1	43.1	0.0
2011	-124.6	69.1	-15.7	41.7	29.5	0.0
2012	-139.4	38.8	2.8	36.2	61.6	0.0
2013	-99.5	34.1	-15.1	3.6	76.9	0.0
2014	-101.7	33.9	-17.9	0.3	85.4	0.0
2015	-80.6	19.5	-25.5	-10.9	101.4	3.9

Source: ONS UK Economic Accounts.

without necessitating damaging domestic adjustments is something in the overseas sector itself – an improvement in the terms of trade, an increase in world demand for our exports, or a lower exchange rate. Of course, the UK has no control, or even much influence, over the first two of these. But it most assuredly does over the third.

If the UK were to enjoy a boost to its net exports (for whatever reason), then the current account deficit would fall and the government deficit would drop, thanks to increased tax receipts and lower government expenditure caused by a higher level of economic activity. Moreover, other things being equal, the financial position of the private sector would improve (as savings rose, thanks to higher income for both households and companies).

The unsustainability of consumer spending

The last serious imbalance in the UK economy is that far too much of what additional demand there has been – even though this has pushed up the growth rate and reduced unemployment – has been the result of increased consumption, which is itself unsustainable. As well as the increase in employment levels (which has raised total income from employment), the extra demand has been fed by increased consumer confidence, an explosion in credit, and a rise in asset prices. Over the period 2000 to 2015, house prices nationally have risen by 140% and in London by 200%. Meanwhile, the increases since 2009 have been 26% and 68% respectively, while between 2009 and 2015 the FTSE 100 index rose by 40%.

The European dimension

It is possible to overdo the gloom and doom about the UK's trading position. After all, a significant part of the problem derives from the weakness of the eurozone, which is still overwhelmingly our largest single trading partner. Indeed, over the last four years, our trade with non-euro countries has improved considerably, to the point where it is now running at a substantial surplus. The overall trade account is only in deficit because we have been running a large and increasing deficit with the eurozone.

There may be certain long-term structural factors that make such a state of affairs – i.e. a deficit with the eurozone and a surplus with the rest of the world – the natural order of things. Even so, two factors have worsened the situation. First, the eurozone has grown extremely slowly compared to most other parts of the world, and certainly compared to the UK. This has limited the growth of its imports – including goods and services produced in the UK.

Indeed, estimates by Capital Economics suggest that if the eurozone had grown in line with the US and the UK then UK exports would have been boosted so much that, other things being equal, the UK could actually now be running an overall trade surplus.

This can be taken encouragingly. After all, if the eurozone returned to rude economic health, the UK might well be able to see a significant trade surplus without needing a lower exchange rate. On the other hand, there is scant prospect of this happening any time soon. Accordingly, UK economic policy has to take the eurozone as it is and this implies the need for a lower exchange rate to generate a much improved trade performance.

Second, although the ECB was slow to adopt a policy of quantitative easing (QE), and slow also to cut interest rates, more recently it has been more overtly expansionary with regard to both interest rates and QE. Given the limited effectiveness of QE operating through the usual domestic channels, this policy has been widely interpreted as a competitive exchange rate strategy. Between January 2007 and February 2016, before Brexit fears really began to build, the pound/euro exchange rate rose by 11%. With the UK growing strongly and not operating any sort of exchange rate policy, this has contributed a substantial amount to the eurozone's recovery. Indeed, its strategy has relied on taking business from the UK, in the eurozone, the UK and third parties. This is indeed a classic case of beggar thy neighbour. And in this instance we are the neighbour. The UK is in sore need of a new policy.

The optimal current account position

In all the discussions about UK economic policy we cannot recall any consideration – in the public or private sector – of what the optimal current account balance is for a country such as the UK. It is widely assumed that about zero is about right – although it seems also to arouse scant anxiety that the UK balance has been nowhere near this point for a long time.

Moreover, plenty of other developed economies are nowhere near it either. Germany is running a current account surplus of 8% of GDP, while the figures for Norway and Switzerland are 6.9% and 7.2% respectively. Although China's surplus has fallen a long way, it is still running at 3% of GDP. Japan's surplus is also 3% of GDP, while Singapore's is a staggering 20% of GDP. Of course, there must also be some substantial deficits to balance these surpluses – and there are. Besides the UK with its deficit of 5.4% in 2015, the US has a deficit of 2.6% and many countries in Africa and Latin America are running large deficits.

Thinking about the developed countries such as Germany, Switzerland, and Singapore, are they so different from the UK that their optimal current account position is radically different from the UK's? And if not, whose is out of kilter: theirs or the UK's? Or both?

The current account and wealth accumulation

The starting point for an analysis of this issue is the realisation that the current account position reflects the difference between national saving and investment. A surplus reflects an excess of domestic saving over domestic investment while a deficit reflects a shortfall. Equally, a current account surplus, as a matter of logic, always has as its counterpart a capital account deficit, that is to say, a flow of capital abroad. Accordingly, other things equal, a current account surplus adds to the stock of national wealth (in the form of real assets abroad, or financial claims on other countries) and a deficit diminishes it (as overseas holdings of real assets or claims on the country increase).

Whether a country should run a surplus or deficit therefore comes down to a decision about the optimum rate of investment (and capital accumulation) and the balance of advantages and disadvantages about having this desired level, whatever it is, financed domestically or by overseas wealth holders, as well as the balance of advantages and disadvantages from accumulating wealth in the form of real assets or paper claims on foreigners as opposed to real assets at home.

The Chinese case

China may provide a useful starting point. It has both a huge level of investment, and a huge level of saving, both close to 50% of GDP, but saving has run ahead of investment, reflected in the current account surplus. It is widely believed that China's investment rate is excessive in that much of the investment is wasteful and the poor returns on it threaten the stability of the banking system.

But if China reduced investment, other things equal, this would both reduce aggregate demand and cause the current account surplus to widen. What China's economy appears to need is reduced saving and increased consumption, both to make up for reduced investment and to close the current account gap. Why is this not the policy of the Chinese authorities? To some extent it is, certainly in their rhetoric. And China's surplus has fallen substantially. But the authorities are concerned to move slowly in case a collapse of investment causes a hard landing in the economy. Nevertheless, there is a suspicion that elements within the authorities have decided that a continued surplus is in China's interest. They may believe that:

(i) Having a strong export sector, building up surpluses, furthers the long-term growth of China's economy;

(ii) Amassing huge foreign exchange reserves puts China in a strong bargaining position vis-vis the rest of the world and gives the Chinese government substantial international clout;

(iii) The huge reserves protect China and its currency from possible instability in the future.

While conceding somewhat on point (iii), most western analysts find China's continued surplus bizarre. Essentially it involves still poor Chinese people saving (i.e. not consuming) in order to allow rich Americans (and others) to spend and consume.

Demographics

Demographic considerations also have a considerable influence on the optimum current account position. Suppose that a country's population is set to age substantially. When this happens, you would expect a substantial swing towards dis-saving as retirees carry on spending even though they are no longer working and producing. In anticipation of this situation, it would be prudent for the country as a whole to build up financial assets through saving. This would take the form of persistent current account surpluses, implying the build-up of net overseas assets. So a country about to undergo a significant ageing of its population might readily run a significant current account surplus at first, counter-balanced subsequently by a significant current account deficit as retirees spend their accumulated capital.

The demographic factor has been a widely used argument to justify Japan's sustained current account surplus. It is sometimes also deployed to justify Germany's and Switzerland's (although it is unclear how well such an argument stands up in their case).

The UK has strong demographics, with the population set to grow considerably. Nevertheless, this cannot justify more than a fraction of the UK's current account deficit.

The UK case

Turning to the UK in more detail, in marked contrast to China, we appear to have an inadequate rate of domestic investment which is not fully funded by domestic saving, hence the current account deficit. Indeed, it is the low rate of saving that is the appropriate marker because the need to draw in savings from abroad to finance such investment as we carry out, reduces the effective rate of capital accumulation, since part of whatever is accumulated is owned, or at least claimed against, by overseas wealth holders.

It is easy to get yourself in a pickle by agonising about the direction of causation behind the accounting identities. Is it low saving that 'causes' the current account deficit, or the current account deficit (i.e. the excess of imports over exports) that causes low saving (because it depresses incomes)? In reality, the relationships are symbiotic. The causation is complex, different between countries and may change over time. But we need not agonise about these complexities.

As regards what needs to change to bring about a satisfactory macroeconomic result for the UK in current circumstances there is no doubt. The last thing we need is to reduce investment, while increased saving (either or both of which would reduce the current account deficit) would, other things equal, reduce aggregate demand and increase unemployment. What is required is a set of policies that reduces or eliminates the current account deficit without depressing aggregate demand.

That means a lower exchange rate than we have been used to – at least until the Brexit vote caused it to drop. Higher exports and/or lower imports would not only reduce the current account deficit but, assuming that there are spare resources in the economy, would also raise GDP and income and hence increase private savings, as well as reducing the fiscal deficit.

No subject for government?

There is a view that, aside from the contribution of their own fiscal policy, governments should take no interest in the current account. The private sector's current account balance is a private matter and governments should leave well alone. Accordingly, if a country runs a current account deficit while the public financial position is balanced – that is to say the current account position is wholly private – then the government should not turn a hair. It is simply none of its business. After all, such a private sector deficit represents the profit and utility maximising decisions of countless 'economic agents' who, acting in their own personal best interests, produce an outcome that is the best possible one for them, given the prevailing circumstances.

Putting the matter slightly differently, with regard to just about all other markets, most economists believe that markets are best left to their own devices. The market prices that are the result of the forces of supply and demand produce the best possible outcome for production and welfare, given the prevailing circumstances. Why should the foreign exchange market be any different?

This argument that balance of payments imbalances don't matter and the foreign exchange market should be left to its own devices is unconvincing, for the following reasons:

(i)   Significant current account deficits often do occur side by side with substantial public deficits (this is currently true in the UK, but this is not always the case);

(ii) Private sector 'agents' take their decisions, including decisions about overseas transactions that then affect the exchange rate, in the context of a panoply of policies set by the government (and central bank);

(iii) It is widely acknowledged that with regard to saving and investment, the private sector cannot always be relied upon to take decisions which are in its best interests. Because of the separation of ownership from control, managements of business enterprises may invest significantly too little. Meanwhile, in regard to their saving behaviour, individuals are notably myopic;

(iv) There is no necessary reason why the self-interested decisions of international asset holders should coincide with our national self-interest;

(v) There is ample evidence that real exchange rates can diverge from the underlying fundamentals for long periods and ample evidence that such divergences can do huge damage;

(vi) The foreign exchange market is different from most other markets because investors and traders do not have a clear view of what the right level is for an exchange rate, and because a misaligned exchange rate can have huge effects on the economy, which then affect the appropriate level of the exchange rate;

(vii) If 'countries' mean anything at all, then governments have a responsibility that goes beyond the self-interest of today's 'economic agents'. If they don't, then what is the point of so much economic policy? If current account deficits do not matter as long as they are 'private', in what sense is it right for governments to strive to boost the rate of economic growth? Why not simply leave it to be determined as the outcome of 'market forces'?

Conclusion

The upshot is that although it might be extremely difficult to pin down the size of the optimum current account surplus or deficit, in the UK's case we may be pretty sure that its current huge deficit is seriously sub-optimal. What's more, bearing in mind the consequences for both the real economy and the financial markets, this is most assuredly something for the policy authorities to be concerned about. Indeed, we suspect that there is scarcely any other country in the developed world (apart possibly from the US, which is a special case) that would have regarded its exchange rate and balance of payments with such blithe insouciance.

3

The historical background to the UK's current account

During the 19th century, Britain had a huge current account surplus, balanced by equally large capital exports. Our surplus was not achieved by Britain enjoying a positive visible trade balance over most of this period. Despite Britain's pre-eminence, at least during the first half of the century, as 'the workshop of the world', the available statistics show Britain generally running a visible trade deficit only partially offset by a surplus in services. The reason why Britain had a major overall current account surplus during the 19th century was that the country enjoyed the benefit of a huge accumulation of net assets abroad, which generated a massive net income.

The beginning of competitiveness problems

The pre-eminence of Britain at least in terms of living standards, up to the outbreak of World War I, therefore relied only to a limited extent on the competiveness of our manufactures. Certainly, for the early decades of the 19th century, Britain enjoyed a major benefit in that there was little international competition for the goods which British industry was making at the time, but this was always a fragile advantage.

Some loss of market share for Britain was inevitable as other countries caught up with the prime mover. Nevertheless, it is difficult to argue that the level of the pound did not contribute to the relatively slow growth in British manufacturing compared to what happened in other countries in the run-up to the First World War.

If Britain was dogged by the strength of sterling up to 1914, worse was to follow when the war was over. Following the precedent set at the end of the Napoleonic Wars, the Cunliffe Committee recommended that the parity between the pound and the dollar should be re-established at the pre-War rate - $4.86 to the pound – even though inflation in Britain had been much higher during the war than in the USA – about 80% in Britain compared to 50% in the USA. This objective was eventually attained in 1925, but at the expense of stagnation during nearly all of the 1920s. By 1931, GDP was still slightly lower than it had been in 1919.

The 1930s, however, told a very different story. In 1931, sterling was allowed to be driven off its previous parity and to fall in value by 31% against the dollar, and by 24% against all other major currencies. The result was a dramatic improvement in the country's economic performance. By 1938 GDP had grown by 24% and manufacturing output by 45%. By the end of the decade, however, after the USA had devalued the dollar by 41% in 1934 and the gold bloc countries had followed suit in 1936, Britain's competitive edge had disappeared and the economy was moving back towards depression, only to be rescued by rearmament as World War II approached. In 1948, the Economic Commission for Europe estimated that sterling was as overvalued in 1938 as it had been in 1929.

Post-war problems

The UK was on the winning side during World War II, but emerged from the conflict heavily over-extended and with its currency yet again substantially over-valued – initially against the US dollar but subsequently against a basket of currencies, including those of many countries recovering strongly from the war. The result was devaluation in 1949 and 1967. Nevertheless, the UK's share of world trade continued to decline remorselessly, from 10.7% in 1950, to 5.7% in 1980, and then to 2.7% by 2010. Again, to some extent this was inevitable as many countries around the world developed rapidly. But the UK also lost market share to countries that were similar to it, particularly Germany.

The China issue

Thanks to a series of reforms begun in 1979, China greatly increased its productive capacity and its role in world trade. Not only did its nominal exchange rate fall but, because of rapid increases in productivity (not offset by rises in the nominal exchange rate), China's real exchange rate fell by some 75% over the next decade, producing an enormous disparity between the costs of manufacturing almost anything in the UK – and indeed in most of the West – compared to China and other countries along the Pacific Rim, most of which also devalued heavily following the 1997 Asian crisis.

Two extremely important consequences have flowed from these developments. The first is that, as a result of the cost base being so much lower in the East than it has been in the West, there has been a huge transfer of manufacturing capacity from the western world to the Pacific Rim.

The cost base is made up of all production costs incurred in the domestic currency. Typically for manufacturing operations, about one third of total costs are for raw materials and plant and machinery, for which there are world prices. The other two thirds is made up of costs incurred in sterling in the UK and renminbi in China – mostly wages, but also including everything from audit charges to taxi fares, from cleaning costs to interest charges, from getting stationery printed to getting vehicles repaired. These costs are all charged out to the rest of the world in the domestic currency and the higher its valuation, via the exchange rate, the more expensive domestic output will appear to be to the rest of the world. It is because the cost base became so much lower in the East than the West that, on a massive scale, manufacturing capacity migrated eastwards.

The second crucial result of this change is that the West – unable to compete with the East over a very wide range of manufacturing output – began to run huge balance of payments deficits with countries such as China. By the 2000s, China was running a current account surplus which averaged about 5% of its GDP for the whole of the decade, peaking at a staggering 10% in 2007, while the USA ran a deficit of 4.5%. During the same decade, the trade deficit between the UK and China averaged about £10bn per annum, but in recent years the overall UK current account position, including the UK's trade balance with China, has deteriorated very sharply.

The overall result has been that the West has become more and more deeply indebted to the East at the same time as the enormous benefit of increased productivity that well-run manufacturing operations always bring in train has generated massive growth rates along the Pacific Rim. Since 2007, the aggregate growth for the last eight years in the West has been not much above zero while in the East it has been close to 77%. In the UK, the economy during these eight years has grown by 7.3%, but the population has increased by 6.5%, so that GDP per head, a good proxy for living standards, has hardly increased at all. In China, by contrast, over the same eight years, GDP has risen by about 93% and GDP per head by almost 85%.

What this brief history of the make-up of UK exports and imports shows is that our performance has always been price sensitive and that the exchange rate has always been a crucial factor in determining what our trading position will be. With occasional exceptions such as in the 1930s, there has been a pronounced tendency for sterling to be too strong, with the consequence that our manufactured exports have tended to be uncompetitive and importing too attractive.

The result has been to make manufacturing in the UK generally unprofitable; to discourage able people from taking up a career making and selling things in the UK; to ensure that we have kept losing our share of world trade; to make us suffer from chronic balance of payments problems; and to discourage investment. Moreover, the overall result has been to make our economy grow more slowly than it should have done as a result of a combination of both deflationary policies to protect the balance of payments and foregoing much of the growth in productivity which a higher contribution from manufacturing would have allowed us to achieve.

There are many reasons why a high value for sterling has been popular in the UK – from holiday makers getting a good rate of exchange for their trips abroad to the City liking a strong exchange rate because it provides those working there with more international leverage. And there are further reasons – discussed later – why policy makers have favoured a strong pound. But the overall impact of our over-valued currency has been to leave our economy much weaker and more unbalanced than it needed to be.

4

How could the current account gap be closed?

If the exchange rate were appreciably lower than it has been in recent years and the UK's trade balance improved substantially, what would be the nature of the exports that now appeared?

A pound is a pound is a pound. In principle, we could close the gap between overseas income and expenditure in several different ways. However, a number of factors, outlined below, suggest that increased manufacturing output, and indeed an increased share of manufacturing in GDP, will have to play an important part.

Productivity and costs

It is important to realise that countries are not competitive simply as a result of wages being low. It is wage costs per unit of output, not wage levels considered in isolation, that are crucial. In economies such as Germany, Japan and Switzerland, hourly wage rates in manufacturing industry are high but because these economies have very large accumulations of capital and skills, output per head is also very high and wages as a component of costs are correspondingly low. This is why it is possible for countries such as Singapore, which also has a well-paid labour force, to remain highly competitive and to continue to grow rapidly – by almost 3% in 2014 and by an average of 6.4% per annum for the last 10 years.

It is true that, as economies get richer, they tend to concentrate production on more complicated products and their industries tend to become more high-tech. This is the result of their growth success, however, and not the cause. That is why it is an illusion for UK policy-makers to believe that moving the UK economy to higher-tech manufacturing will make us more competitive. This will tend to happen as we succeed but we cannot jump several stages of development in one go.

While we await our 'high-tech transformation', the UK simply cannot produce enough high-tech exports to enable it to pay its way in the world. Moreover, although high-tech is more difficult than low- or medium-tech to attack from low cost base economies, it is not impossible. In the long-term, high-tech is likely to be almost as vulnerable as less sophisticated industries as the Chinese learn to build aircraft and their engines, the Indians to produce world class drugs and the Koreans to produce better cars.

In the medium term, therefore, if the UK is ever to get its balance of payments problems under control, we will have both to nurture those industries we still retain and to re-establish more medium-tech activity. There is no knowing the industry structure that would best enable the UK to return to something like current account balance. But it seems likely that, bearing in mind the structure of UK exports, balance in our current account would require manufacturing as a proportion of UK GDP to get back to somewhere around 15% of GDP. To do this, we will have to have a much lower exchange rate than we have been used to.

The service sector to the rescue?

There are two well-worn counter-arguments to this approach. One is that, because we are better at producing services than manufactured goods, we should put our effort behind developing our service industries where we have a competitive advantage. The other is that we should move up market into high-skilled occupations and thus be able to keep sufficiently far ahead of world competition to keep paying our way. We consider these two arguments in turn.

The UK is good at producing services and selling them on world markets – and it always has been. Financial services, including insurance, banking, legal and accounting services and ship broking – as well as other invisible export earnings from tourism and intellectual property – are responsible for the UK having a large services export surplus every year – £89bn in 2015, but averaging £59bn per annum for the previous 10 years.

This has happened partly by luck – the pre-eminence of English as the world's business language and our position geographically in the world half way between the USA and the Far East – and partly by good management. The UK has a reliable legal system, a long accumulated depth of expertise and an attractive environment all of which have stood its service industries in good stead. Services are also, in general, less price sensitive than manufactured goods because they are less easy to compare. There is, therefore, everything to be said for protecting and enhancing the UK's services exports wherever we reasonably can.

The problem is that most exports – even for the UK – are not services but goods and it is extremely difficult –

and indeed historical experience has shown it to be impossible – to close the gap between our export surplus on services and our deficit on goods solely by increasing services exports. Our visible deficit was £126bn in 2015 and an average of £97bn for the previous 10 years, with the corresponding figures for the overall trade deficit being £39bn and an average of £38bn for the previous decade.

Relatedly, does moving upmarket with a better educated and trained labour force look as though it might solve our trade deficit problem, through both helping to bolster still further our service sector and helping us to produce more high-end manufactured output? Despite the obvious intuitive appeal that it would, it is hard to see how it might happen in a way which would make more than a marginal difference in the relevant time-frame. And, in the long-run, better educational and training standards will only improve our competitive position if they are not accompanied by higher earnings expectations. The situation might be a bit better on services, some of which, at least, depend more than manufacturing on the intellectual capacity of the workforce, but it is difficult to see there being a quantum leap in net trade performance as a result.

Actually, what has happened is that for many decades, the lack of profitability and the poor prospects in manufacturing have led to low earnings and low prestige, with the result that this vital sector of our economy has been starved of talent. Faced with a poisonous mixture of poor management and unmanageable competition, UK industry, especially its low- and medium-tech varieties, has withered and declined. This is the price paid by economies whose exchange rate is too high for its manufacturing industries to bear. The trade deficits thus generated require deflationary policies to contain. Investment as a proportion of GDP declines. Economic growth is reduced.

A less dramatic answer

All that said, it shouldn't be forgotten that with a lower exchange rate there are all sorts of ways that net exports might recover without a dramatic turnaround in the UK's industrial structure. We could achieve the result, or at least part of it, simply by expanding the production and sales abroad of those things where we already have a significant presence.

Motor cars are a good example. There is no reason to suppose that the demand for particular brands/types of cars is not price sensitive to some degree. If sterling were maintained at an appreciably lower rate than it has been then British exports of cars would be higher – and, just as importantly, for the same reason, our imports of cars would be lower.

This leads on to a more general point. Improving the trade balance can be achieved just as effectively through reduced imports as it can through increased exports. Of course, we are not going to suddenly start producing bananas to substitute for the imported variety. But in many cases we both produce domestically and import broadly similar products. Cars are not the only example. Moving down the value-added chain, take bottled mineral water as an example. Or, with admittedly more product discrimination, cheese.

Nor does effective substitution of domestic for foreign have to involve the whole product. It may simply mean more of a production process being conducted domestically as opposed to abroad.

For example, it has recently been suggested that Rolls-Royce may relocate some of its production processes abroad, including to India because of lower costs. If the sterling exchange rate were substantially lower, such pressure would be appreciably reduced.

Naturally, where producers need to switch the sourcing for their output from abroad to here in the UK – and even more so if they are to decide to relocate whole areas of production here – they need more than a transitory move of the exchange rate to encourage them to do so. Accordingly, time lags are likely to be significant, and probably longer than in the past before a response is forthcoming. Moreover, the response will be greater the more the producers believe that the new exchange rate will be long-lived. They are more likely to take this view if a competitive exchange rate is an avowed policy objective. (More on this below.)

Another twist on services

Some of the adjustment can also come from services. It is widely believed that services exports are not very price-sensitive. That may be true of some services but not all. It is difficult to believe, for instance, that our net tourism balance would not improve as a result of a substantial drop in the exchange rate, thereby making UK holidays cheaper compared to foreign alternatives, for both UK and foreign holiday-makers alike.

But suppose it is true that the demand for UK service exports is not particularly price sensitive. Accordingly, after a devaluation of sterling the profit maximising option for UK service providers would be to keep the foreign currency price the same, thereby yielding a higher sterling price. Meanwhile, with regard to our imports of manufactured goods, which are price sensitive, the profit-maximising decision for importers might well be to keep the sterling price unchanged, implying a drop in the foreign currency price. If this happened then, although UK trade volumes might not respond to the lower exchange rate, there would be an improvement in the terms of trade which, in regard to its effect on the trade balance, would be just as good.

Whether something like this will happen would depend on the competitive conditions in the UK's service exporting businesses. To the extent that these industries are oligopolistic then something like the above result should stand. If these industries are fully competitive, however, then the foreign currency prices should be competed down, leaving the sterling prices (more or less) unaltered and thereby risking a terms of trade loss, which would serve to worsen the trade balance.

The exchange rate and the investment income balance

The UK has a huge balance sheet, with overseas assets and domestic liabilities to overseas asset holders each of the order of 500% of GDP. The assets, and the income on them, are predominantly denominated in foreign currencies, while the liabilities, and the payments made on them, are largely in sterling. In other words, the UK is 'long' on foreign currencies.

Accordingly, a depreciation raises the sterling value of income flows from abroad, while leaving the sterling value of payments to overseas asset holders unchanged. Alternatively, you could say that the depreciation leaves the foreign currency value of the income flows on our assets unchanged, while diminishing the foreign currency value of the payments we send overseas.

If the amounts of assets and liabilities are the same, and the returns earned on assets are the same as those paid on liabilities (it won't be), then, supposing that the return is 2%, with assets and liabilities of 500% of GDP, a 20% fall of sterling would bring about a boost to our investment income balance of 2% of GDP (500% x 20% x 2%) – about £36bn.

Trade, growth, productivity and inequality

To what extent is our weak trade performance responsible for our relatively low rate of productivity increase, economic growth and living standards, and the rises we have seen in both socio-economic and regional inequality? Why has our performance in these key respects been so much worse than in many other parts of the world? What does the differing performance of other countries have to tell us?

Evidence from across the planet shows that there is a pattern which we decline to follow at our peril. Economies, large and small, which have grown quickly – and which are still doing so – perform best when they have strong export-orientated manufacturing sectors. There are exceptions – countries in the Middle East, for instance, whose wealth comes from natural resources such as oil – but these countries tend to be relatively poorly diversified and to suffer from extremes of inequality.

The countries which offer all their populations the best outcomes and which appear to have the most secure future prosperity are those whose economies are based on a wide variety of manufacturing industries, supporting a thriving service sector, with increasing demand in the economy unconstrained by balance of payments problems. These are the conditions which led to the huge increase in prosperity in continental Europe between 1950 and 1970, which prevailed in Japan until the 1980s and which drove the rise in prosperity for many years in the Asian Tiger economies – South Korea, Hong Kong, Taiwan and Singapore. They are still very evident in China today and indeed in many of the other economies stretched out along the Pacific Rim.

With slow growth goes increasing inequality. It is no coincidence that relatively slow growing, heavily service orientated economies, such as the USA and the UK, have some of the highest indices of inequality and that these have become more pronounced in recent years.

Part Two

Exchange Rates and
Exchange Rate Policy

5

How British exchange rate policy has evolved over the last 100 years

Over the last 100 years, UK exchange rate policy has veered between obsessive control and benign (or malign) neglect. During the 19th century, the UK was at the centre of the gold standard, which was a fixed exchange rate system between different currencies, based upon each currency's fixed link with gold. This system severely constrained domestic policy. Indeed, monetary policy hardly existed in any independent sense, while fiscal policy was constrained by the perceived need to pay down the national debt. In order to maintain the fixed link, when gold was draining out of the Bank of England, the Bank had to raise interest rates. And when it was pouring in, it had the scope to cut them.

A critical decision

This system came to an end with the suspension of gold convertibility during the First World War. In 1925, however, the then Chancellor of the Exchequer, Winston Churchill, was persuaded that it was essential that the UK should return to the gold standard at the pre-war parity, notwithstanding the fact that in the interim, UK costs and prices had risen faster than their equivalents abroad. This condemned the country to a prolonged period of deflation and depression. The general strike of 1926 was a direct result of this policy decision.

Keynes lambasted it in his pamphlet *The Economic Consequences of Mr Churchill*, so titled to chime in with his international best-seller, *The Economic Consequences of the Peace*, a devastating critique of the Versailles peace treaty at the end of the First World War.

This exchange rate policy of Churchill's – adopted, with some misgivings by the great man, on the advice of Treasury and Bank of England officials – can be seen as the first of a series of British establishment decisions which put the objective of financial stability – and the supposed interests of the City of London – above the objective of international competitiveness and the interests of the wider economy outside the Square Mile.

Putting the economic situation then in today's economic parlance, the UK's faster rate of inflation during the First World War had raised its real exchange rate. A lower nominal rate to offset the higher inflation, and therefore return the real rate to where it had been earlier, might have seemed appropriate. Instead, however, the former nominal rate was adhered to, which implied a policy of austerity and deflation to reduce costs and prices in order to push the real exchange rate back to where it had been. In other words, the British authorities had chosen a policy of 'internal devaluation'. This has been mirrored, almost a century later, in the policies adopted within the eurozone to try to make its peripheral countries competitive again, without recourse to exchange rate devaluation, which would require a break-up of the euro.

The lessons of the 1930s

In 1931, however, matters came to a head. It wasn't so much a case of the government deciding that the gold standard parity was no longer worth adhering to, but rather a case of it finding that the current position was no longer sustainable. The UK was effectively forced off the gold standard, not knowing what disasters might ensue.

What ensued, thanks to a lower exchange rate and very low interest rates, was the fastest period of economic growth in our industrial history. As one Labour minister said at the time of the gold standard exit: 'No one told us that we could do that.' This experience was to be repeated some sixty years later when the pound was ejected from the ERM (see below.)

Such was the UK's weight in the global economy then that many other countries immediately followed sterling's lead to leave the gold standard. Others followed later. As a result, the 1930s became a period of exchange rate instability. It is often alleged that this resulted from countries trying to gain advantage over each other through 'competitive devaluation'. In the context of depressed demand – a problem that had begun in America with the Wall Street Crash of 1929, but which was intensified by the global financial crisis of 1931 – countries could bolster their own position by gaining a greater share of markets, both at home and abroad.

In practice, though, most countries were forced into devaluation when they lost control of monetary and exchange rate policy. One notable exception is Germany which, under the economic leadership of Hjalmar Schacht, actively sought to gain competitive advantage by operating with a lower exchange rate.

Hand in hand with currency instability went protectionist trade policies. The result was a major contraction of global trade. Essentially, the open trading system that had characterised the first era of globalisation, before the First World War, collapsed.

The return to fixed exchange rates – and the relapse

At the end of World War II, John Maynard Keynes was keen to ensure that the post-war world would not be damaged by the exchange rate instability and protectionism that had characterised the 1930s. Accordingly, together with his US counterpart, Harry Dexter White, he set about constructing a post-war economic regime that would provide for fixed, but adjustable, exchange rates. This Bretton Woods system (named after the hotel in New Hampshire where it was concocted) lasted from 1946 until 1971. Afterwards, the pound, in common with other currencies, floated.

At first, governments welcomed the sense of freedom that floating exchange rates seemed to bring. At last they could set domestic policy in pursuit of domestic objectives without fear of the consequences for the balance of payments, or the reaction in the foreign exchange markets.

But this freedom coincided with the onset of high inflation. Some economists would argue this was due to the operation of lax monetary and fiscal policy in the context of over-full employment; others would point to the oil price hikes of 1973/4 and the role of trade unions. Whatever the relative weight of these two explanations, the phenomenon of high inflation, higher than anything that had been experienced in developed economies except for brief periods during the Napoleonic Wars, the First World War and the Korean War, convinced both academic economists and policy-makers that the world needed some sort of nominal anchor. If not gold – and very few wanted a return to the 'barbarous relic' – or some sort of fixed exchange rate system, then what?

Monetarism triumphant – for a time

The first port of call was the monetary aggregates, in some shape or form. This was far from accidental. The arch-advocate of floating exchange rates, Milton Friedman, was also the high priest of monetarism. He advocated fixed annual targets for the rate of increase of the money supply. His thinking provided the intellectual ballast for a completely new macroeconomic policy, focused on control of the money supply.

In contrast to popular opinion, the adoption of some form of monetarism in the UK began before the advent of Mrs Thatcher's government. In 1976, the Chancellor of the Exchequer, Denis Healey, adopted a money supply framework. When the Conservatives took power in 1979, they installed a formal target for the growth of the monetary aggregate called Sterling M3.

What ensued was one of the most ideologically driven bouts of economic policy in the UK's history. Some proponents and defenders of the government's monetarist policies argued that the exchange rate didn't matter. It was merely a relative price. The work of getting inflation to fall was to be done by the significant planned reduction in the growth rate of the money supply (defined as £M3).

Paradoxically, at the same time, others, including the government's Chief Economic Adviser, Terry (now Lord) Burns, saw a strong exchange rate as absolutely vital to bringing inflation down. It was the tool through which a tough monetary policy did its work. These two positions were, of course, polar opposites. Nevertheless, their proponents could unite behind the idea that the sharp rise of the pound was nothing to worry about, still less to take policy action to resist.

From today's perspective, three key points (that were perceived at the time by the present co-authors) are clear to almost all economists:

- Control of the money supply had next to nothing to do with the reduction of inflation by Mrs Thatcher's first government – not least because the money supply was not tightly controlled. The government discovered that it could declare monetary targets until it was blue in the face but what actually happened to the money supply was determined in the private sector, and especially in the banks.

- This did not matter for the achievement of low inflation because the high interest rates deemed necessary for the control of the money supply, and the concomitant surge of the pound, buoyed also by North Sea Oil, did the job anyway.

- Opinions will differ as to whether this was necessary and/or desirable, but the result of this policy was a major collapse of manufacturing activity and indeed a substantial fallback in the UK's long-term manufacturing capacity. The UK's already sharp fall in manufacturing's share of GDP plumbed new depths – but subsequently continued further (see Figure 6).

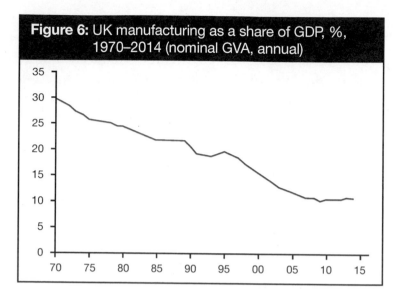

Figure 6: UK manufacturing as a share of GDP, %, 1970–2014 (nominal GVA, annual)

The interregnum

Eventually the penny dropped – and so did the pound. For a time the government dabbled with the idea that monetarism was basically sound; it was merely that it had adopted the wrong definition of the money supply. A panoply of other monetary aggregates followed, each in time abandoned in favour of some new concoction, but bringing no greater reliability. After a while, it became clear that the game was up and quietly the government downgraded, and then abandoned, monetarism.

So it was that, having effectively ditched monetarism at some point in the 1980s, the UK authorities were left with the familiar problem of what to use as an anchor for nominal values. Surprise, surprise, they opted for the exchange rate. In 1987, Nigel Lawson, the then Chancellor of the Exchequer, began a policy of covertly shadowing the Deutschemark, although this exchange rate policy was subsequently abandoned after strong opposition from the Prime Minister.

In 1990 this exchange rate policy was taken to its logical conclusion when Lawson's successor, John Major, took sterling into the European Exchange Rate Mechanism (ERM), the forerunner of the euro. In the by now familiar pattern, the UK authorities had a serious problem with inflation, which had risen significantly. Accordingly, it was thought necessary to fix the pound at a rate against the Deutschemark that would bear down on inflation. Unfortunately, of course, as before, it would also bear down on the UK economy, and on exporters in particular.

For two years until the pound's ejection from the ERM in September 1992, UK macroeconomic policy was dominated by the overriding requirement to keep the pound in its designated fluctuation band against the Deutschemark. The result was that the authorities effectively had no freedom to set an independent monetary policy. Even though the UK housing market was in the midst of a meltdown, interest rates had to be kept high to protect sterling's position in the ERM. In other words, the authorities were in exactly the same position that their equivalents had found themselves in sixty years earlier. And, once again, they were delivered from this mess by escape from the exchange rate constraint.

The emergence of inflation targets

Nevertheless, it did not feel like an escape when sterling was ejected from the ERM on September 16th 1992. Indeed, the UK authorities were in a funk. They were in no mood to embrace any other form of exchange rate target. Nevertheless, they needed some sort of nominal anchor. Bearing in mind the experience of the 1980s, going back to monetary targets was not an attractive option. What on earth should they do? They opted for inflation targets.

Inflation targeting was really an adaptation of monetarism. Whereas the latter had pre-supposed a reliable link between an intermediate variable, i.e. the money supply (however defined), and the price level, and recommended targets for the growth of this variable, given the experience of huge monetary instability and the likely unreliability of any monetary aggregate designated as a target, inflation targeting simply by-passed this intermediate stage and set targets for the ultimate policy objective, namely the rate of increase of the price level, i.e. inflation.

In the event, for about 15 years, the inflation targeting regime worked pretty well. Certainly, the inflation rate remained very low, and indeed, close to the target, albeit accompanied by largely anaemic rates of economic growth.

But then came the financial crisis. Afterwards, it came to be believed that the inflation targeting regime had contributed to the previous financial boom and subsequent crash, since, provided that inflation stayed low, the regime obliged the monetary authorities to keep interest rates low, even though signs of financial excess were building up. Moreover, with economic policy focussed exclusively on the inflation rate, the policy regime paid no attention to the maintenance of a competitive exchange rate.

More recently, it has become abundantly clear that with inflation significantly subdued, if not conquered, the obsessive pursuit of inflation targets without concern for other desiderata is damaging. When inflation is public enemy number one it makes a certain amount of sense to put inflation targets centre-stage. Moreover, in some simple views of the world, if the authorities get the inflation rate reliably under control, everything else falls into place. Yet the financial crisis of 2008/9 surely taught us that:

(a) Low and stable inflation is not the be-all and end-all;

(b) Setting interest rates solely in relation to the immediate prospects for inflation can be profoundly destabilising for the financial system, indeed even for the medium-term outturn for inflation;

(c) Evidently, the markets do not always 'know best'. Indeed, for their own sakes, as well as for ours, they need to be saved from their own excesses.

Interestingly, although there has been a shift in the climate of opinion towards the policy authorities needing to exercise some surveillance over the financial system's valuations for equities, bonds, property and other financial instruments, and not just as an input into the determination of inflation, no such conclusion has been embraced about the exchange rate – except as an input into the determination of inflation.

The pound's roller-coaster ride

Since 1992 the pound has been on a rollercoaster ride, as the markets have gyrated from one extreme to the other, with next to no guidance from the policy authorities, let alone intervention, as to where the exchange rate should be.

Initially, the pound sank to a much more competitive level. Moreover, to the surprise of most commentators and the authorities – but not the authors of this pamphlet – the lower exchange rate was not offset by a sharp rise in domestic costs and prices. Not surprisingly, the UK economy responded with one of its best periods of well-balanced and sustainable growth spurts – albeit helped by a revival of the global economy.

This came to an end in 1997. The pound started to rise well before the election of the Labour government in 1997 but it carried on afterwards. Then, as Figure 7 shows, the pound enjoyed a period of remarkable stability, lasting about a decade. But this was stability at the wrong level, as evidenced by the UK's growing current account deficit.

The pound then plunged again in 2008/9, taking it even lower than the levels experienced after 1992. But this was comparatively short-lived. After a few years, the pound was on the rise again and it had lost more than half of the improvement in competitiveness gained after 2008/9 up to the point at which Brexit worries started to build. After the Brexit vote, the pound fell sharply.

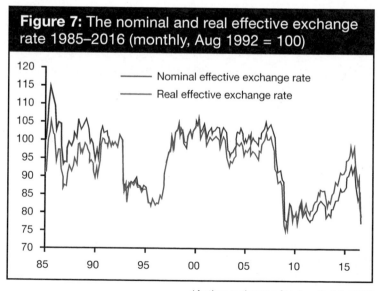

Figure 7: The nominal and real effective exchange rate 1985–2016 (monthly, Aug 1992 = 100)

*Author estimates for Jun. & Jul. 2016

During the last 24 years, despite these major moves in the pound's value, and despite continuing belief in the pound's importance for the economy, chastened by their experience in the ERM in 1990-92, the UK authorities stood well back from anything that smacked of an exchange rate policy. The prevailing wisdom was that:

(a) It was impossible for the authorities to know what the exchange rate should be;

(b) Nevertheless, this wisdom is available to the markets. They know best;

(c) If the markets were to be wrong, there is no way in which the exchange rate could plausibly be corrected.

So, mirroring the so-called Greenspan doctrine about bubbles in financial markets, the conclusion was drawn that the government should leave the exchange rate solely to the market. Accordingly, whereas for much of our history, the exchange rate has provided the lodestar for economic management, over the last quarter century it has been left hanging in the wind. It is just one of the factors, along with things like the growth of consumer credit and the latest Bank of England agents' reports on the state of confidence, and umpteen other factors, to be taken into account when setting interest rates.

Admittedly, circumstances change over time. Nevertheless, one can't help thinking that if it has sometimes been deemed overwhelmingly important to keep the exchange rate at some reasonable level in relation to the UK's economic fundamentals, leaving it to go hang must be a case of going from one misguided extreme to another. It is a case of malign neglect.

It would be instructive to see how other countries view their exchange rates. Do they simply leave them to 'market forces'? Or is this another example of British eccentricity?

6

Other countries' attitudes to exchange rate management, past and present

By and large, since the collapse of the Bretton Woods semi-fixed exchange rate regime in 1971, most countries' economic policies have still put the exchange rate centre-stage. In some cases, they have operated fairly rigid exchange rate policies; in others they have merely attributed a great deal of importance to the exchange rate when setting policy. But in very few cases have they been indifferent to it.

The American exception

The single biggest exception is the United States, which has a continental economy, and has traditionally had comparatively low exposure to international trade. (Even now, exports account for only about 13% of US GDP, and imports about 15%.) Moreover, as the dollar is the world's money, when the US has experienced substantial current account disequilibrium, of the sort that would have destabilised many an ordinary currency, the consequences for it have been far from dramatic. Accordingly, the exchange rate has not figured large in American policy discussions.

This is not to say, however, that it does not matter at all. In particular, from time to time the US authorities have become especially concerned about the supposed undervaluation of the currencies of countries with which the US was in close competition – Germany, Japan, and now China. But the exchange rate has never been as important for the US as it is for many other countries.

Outside the US, for almost every other country the exchange rate has been at the very centre of economic policy. For many small countries, the appropriate policy has been to peg, or at least closely manage, their own currencies against the US dollar. Even for bigger countries, like China and Japan, getting the exchange rate at the right level has been fundamental to the management of economic policy.

In Japan, although the country's obligations to the G7 and various concomitant diplomatic niceties prevent it from openly saying this, aiming for a weaker yen is a key part of its current government's strategy for increasing the inflation rate as a way of bringing economic recovery. What's more, other governments, including those of Japan's G7 partners, have apparently accepted this strategy.

As for China, throughout the period of its industrialisation and rise to global power status it has managed the exchange rate. Most observers would go further: since the Asian financial crisis of 1997, it has deliberately sought to keep the exchange rate undervalued so as to boost the performance of Chinese exports and ensure a large current account surplus. As Figure 8 shows, it has succeeded in achieving this goal. And Figure 9 attests to the concomitant success in amassing huge foreign exchange reserves, built up by the persistent selling of renminbi for foreign currencies.

The German illusion

Interestingly, much the same has been true of Germany, pretty much throughout the post-war period – although you would not think so from reading the financial press. The predominant view is that since the establishment of the Deutschemark in 1948, the German authorities either did not care about the exchange rate or welcomed currency strength. The evident success of the German economy, despite the tendency for the Deutschemark to rise on the exchanges, has been taken by many as confirmation that the German authorities a) didn't care about the exchange rate and b) didn't need to.

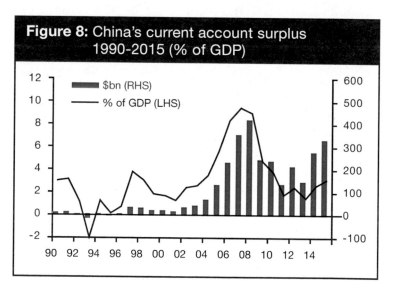

Figure 8: China's current account surplus 1990-2015 (% of GDP)

The truth is exactly the opposite. When the Deutschemark was established in 1948, it was significantly undervalued. The western allies were keen to ensure that the German economy recovered, and

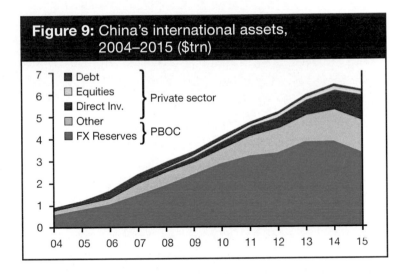

Figure 9: China's international assets, 2004–2015 ($trn)

export success was a key part of this. The subsequent tendency of the Deutschemark to rise – often because other currencies fell – does not promote a case for the irrelevance of the exchange rate. All along, the exchange rate strengthened *behind* Germany's economic success – on exports, productivity growth and cost control. The result is that Germany's *real* exchange rate never reached challenging levels.

Indeed, despite appearances, the Bundesbank was desperately anxious that this should be so. Monetarist in appearance, this institution was in reality a closet 'exchange rate' central bank, of the classic type. Interestingly, this position has continued under the euro. With the exchange rate fixed between Germany and its European competitors, if Germany outperformed in the containment of domestic costs, it would improve its competitiveness, even if the euro held steady. If the euro weakened then German competitiveness would improve still more. This is exactly what has happened, with the result that the German current account surplus is now running at about 8% of GDP.

What has happened to the German surplus is testament to the power of exchange rates. Before the advent of the euro, there was always a tendency for Germany to run surpluses, but this was kept in check by the tendency of the Deutschemark to rise and for other currencies to fall. The record speaks for itself. As Figure 10 shows, between 1970 and 1998, the last year of the Deutschemark, the average German current account surplus was less than 1% of GDP. From 1999, the first year of the euro, until 2014, the average German current account surplus was 4%. In 2015 it was over 8%.

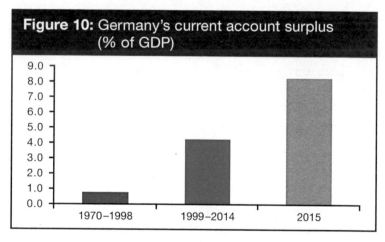

Figure 10: Germany's current account surplus (% of GDP)

Moreover, this change in Germany's current account position is mirrored by a change in the behaviour of its consumers. Before the advent of the euro, despite the myth that German consumers never spend and run very high savings rates, in fact the growth of German consumer spending was roughly in line with the Anglo-Saxon economies, the US and the UK. By contrast, from the advent of the euro in 1999 to 2014, although things perked up in 2015, the average rate of increase of German consumer spending has been just over ½%, compared to over 2% in 1970-1998 (see Figure 11).

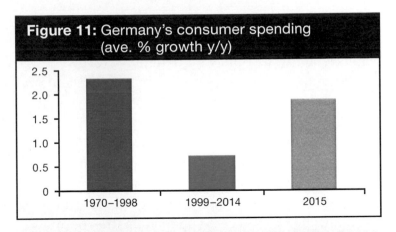

Figure 11: Germany's consumer spending (ave. % growth y/y)

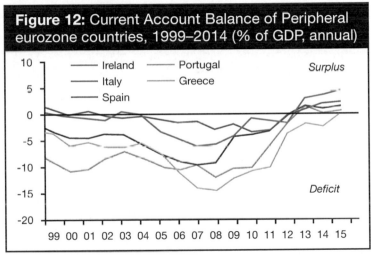

Figure 12: Current Account Balance of Peripheral eurozone countries, 1999–2014 (% of GDP, annual)

Peripheral Europe

The five peripheral economies of the eurozone – Ireland, Portugal, Spain, Italy and Greece – also provide ample evidence of the power of exchange rates. After joining the monetary union they carried on inflating faster than core Europe, led by Germany. The result was a sharp deterioration in their current account performance, as shown in Figure 12. The subsequent recession diminished the deficits – and in some cases turned them into surpluses – but this merely transferred the problem from the external accounts to the state of the domestic economy.

Subsequently, as domestic deflation proceeded, the evidence is that in some cases – notably Ireland and Spain – there has been a distinct improvement in competitiveness which has produced the classic response of an improvement in trading performance. This does not contradict the thrust of this pamphlet. Far from it. Our contention is that exchange rates are central to economic performance and should be central to economic policy. What happened in the peripheral members of the eurozone is that their real exchange rate appreciated significantly in the early years of euro membership, thanks to rapid growth of domestic wages and prices, and then subsequently depreciated again, thanks to domestic deflation. This performance is testament to the power of real exchange rates, not the opposite.

The debate about management of the real rate through nominal exchange rate management versus fluctuations in the domestic price level is another issue. We would argue that a policy of domestic deflation to regain competitiveness is both slow and dangerous. The domestic deflation in the peripheral countries has worsened the debt ratios of those countries. It remains to be seen how their economic predicaments pan out. For our purposes here, though, the critical thing is the demonstration that real exchange rates really matter.

Exchange rate policy

Under Mario Draghi, President of the ECB, although the eurozone's central bank was initially slow to loosen monetary policy, more recently it has implicitly pursued a policy of depreciation. The policy was not so called, of course, but this was its purpose. For the evidence should by now be fairly clear that in a broken financial system, quantitative easing (QE) does not work very well through the conventional domestic channels. What it may do, however, provided that other countries are not operating the policy to the same degree, is to put downward pressure on the exchange rate. This is certainly what appears to have happened in the case of the euro, which, since January 2008, has weakened against the dollar by 32%.

This weaker exchange rate will have been welcomed by the ECB for two reasons:

(i) It will have delivered a temporary boost to the inflation rate and thereby helped to stave off the threat of deflation and, for, any given level of nominal interest rates, it will have reduced the real rate of interest;

(ii) It will have boosted eurozone net exports and thereby increased aggregate demand, with all the usual beneficial effects, including on employment.

As it happens, the statistics suggest that this policy – aided and abetted by domestic deflation in the peripheral countries – has worked. The eurozone's current account position has moved from a deficit of $223 bn in 2008 to a surplus of $365bn in 2015. What has happened is that with regard to the roles of external surpluses and domestic demand the whole eurozone has been turning Germanic. Interestingly, despite the G7's apparent forbidding of an explicit exchange rate policy, three of its European members – Germany, France and Italy – have been allowed to get away with an implicit policy amounting to much the same thing.

Meanwhile, the G7's second largest member, Japan, has been trying to do much the same (although, recently, without much success.) Of the G7's members only the US, UK and Canada have not been aiming to boost their economies through a lower exchange rate.

In the rest of the world, exchange rate targeting is common. Hong Kong's currency, of course, is pegged to the US dollar, while Singapore's is managed according to a basket of currencies. In other Asian economies, a managed float regime is operated. In the Middle East, the oil exporters manage their currencies in relation to the dollar. In Africa, South Africa operates a free float, Nigeria a managed float and Morocco a currency peg. In Latin America, Brazil operates a free float, Argentina a managed float and Bolivia a currency peg. In Australia, the RBA operates a floating exchange rate policy.

Reasons for doubting the importance of real exchange rates

Over the last couple of decades – i.e. during a period of British (malign) neglect of the exchange rate – it has become common for economists and others to believe that exchange rates (nominal and real) have become less important as a determinant of trade flows and therefore that their comparative unimportance as a determinant of UK policy does not matter much.

There are two good reasons for believing that exchange rates may now be less important than they were; (a) the increasing importance of trade in services, which are less price sensitive; (b) the increased importance of global supply chains in manufacturing, which may render even trade in manufactures less sensitive to exchange rate changes.

But the evidence is that these two concerns are seriously overdone. The sensitivity of trade performance to exchange rate changes was recently examined in an IMF study ('Exchange rates and Trade Flows: Disconnected?' Global Economic Outlook, May 2015). Its main conclusions were:

(i) A 10% real effective depreciation in a country's currency is associated with a rise of, on average, 1.5% of GDP;

(ii) The boost is found to be the largest in countries with a high initial degree of slack, and where domestic financial systems are operating normally;

(iii) There is some evidence that the rise of global supply chains has weakened the effect of exchange rate changes. However, the bulk of international trade still consists of conventional trade and there is little evidence of a general trend towards disconnect between exchange rates and total exports and imports.

Recent evidence

Nor does the notion that trade flows are no longer very sensitive to exchange rates gel very well with the recent experience of the world's two largest economies, the USA and the eurozone. Since January 2007 the dollar/euro exchange rate has increased by 28%. The dollar's trade-weighted index has risen by 30% and the euro's has fallen by 14%. The results are plain to see in the US trade balance, and worry about the effect of the strong US dollar on US trade was a leading factor behind the Fed's reluctance to raise interest rates during 2015.

Meanwhile, (admittedly aided by depressed domestic demand in countries using the single currency) the eurozone has moved from deficit to surplus as even the weaker, peripheral economies of the monetary union have been forced to become Teutonic in their spending and saving habits, and in their search for GDP growth through competitive internal devaluation.

7

Is it possible to vary the real exchange rate by changing the nominal rate?

In order to have any effect on a country's trading performance it is not enough for the exchange rate – the nominal rate – to be lower. The real rate, that is the nominal rate adjusted for changes in the price level, must be lower also. In other words, the rise in the general level of prices that sometimes follows a depreciation of the currency must not advance so far as to equal the amount by which the exchange rate has fallen. If that happens then the real exchange rate will not have fallen at all and accordingly no lasting benefit to economic performance can be expected – except anything that derives from a burst of higher inflation, which may end up being more than a burst, as the higher inflation comes to be expected and becomes ingrained. (More likely, of course, this burst of higher inflation will bring welfare losses, for all the usual reasons.)

Indeed, given the time lags involved there may not even be any fleeting benefit. After a currency depreciation, it takes time for households and firms to adapt their behaviour to the new set of relative prices. Moreover, depreciation often leads to a deterioration in the terms of trade (the ratio of export prices to import prices) so that the country's real income falls.

Accordingly, you can readily imagine circumstances when, following a depreciation, inflation proceeds so rapidly that the initial fall in the real exchange rate has been wiped out before it has had time to bring any benefits.

Equally, there are cases when a depreciation brings hardly any increase in the general price level – or even a decrease – as higher output brings lower average costs and increased investment. Sometimes any initial upward impulse to the price level may also be offset by reductions in indirect taxes (such as VAT).

Sorting out how inflation in the UK is likely to develop following a drop in the UK nominal exchange rate – such as the one that occurred after the UK's Brexit vote – is key to understanding whether the lower currency will do anything to improve the trade balance and boost GDP. This requires a brief trot through some theoretical considerations and a review of the empirical evidence.

Exchange rates in theory

There are many factors that should influence a country's equilibrium real exchange rate, and these factors are changing over time. Accordingly, the equilibrium rate is liable to change over time. In general, the more successful a country is in producing things (and non-things) that the rest of the world wants to buy then, other things equal, the higher will be its equilibrium real exchange rate. Countries that move from a state of under-development experience a rise in their real exchange rates. Countries that experience a loss of overseas markets, or a fall in the price of their leading exports, undergo a fall in their equilibrium exchange rates.

But the word 'equilibrium' should be treated with care. Economists usually take the equilibrium exchange rate to mean the exchange rate that will give rough balance in a country's overseas trade, while the domestic economy is at 'full employment'. But it may be appropriate for countries sometimes to run sustained surpluses, and for other countries, or the same countries at other times, to run sustained deficits.

Moreover, the full employment condition is not always obvious to identify. After all, there is a mini-industry at work trying to estimate the size of the output gap, or, in other words, the amount of under-employment of resources, including labour but also comprising other factors of production. If there is a higher output gap than previously estimated then aggregate demand needs to be stronger to eliminate this gap and achieve full employment of resources, and thereby realise maximum possible output. Other things being equal this would raise the level of imports and probably require a lower exchange rate to achieve balanced trade.

A country may operate with a real exchange rate well above its equilibrium rate for a prolonged period. This may occur because the economy operates for an extended time below full employment. Or it may operate below its equilibrium rate because of the constellation of government policies. A policy to prevent capital inflows and/or stimulate outflows would deliver this result. Equally, if the government ran a very restrictive fiscal policy (perhaps in order to reduce the ratio of government debt to GDP) this would, other things being equal, decrease the level of GDP and justify a lower real exchange rate in order to achieve full employment.

It is worth asking why, if the equilibrium real exchange rate is higher or lower than the existing rate, the market does not deliver that result itself, either by forcing changes in the nominal rate, or by bringing about changes in the price level that, for any given level of the nominal exchange rate, change the real rate.

The answer is that there is such a mechanism in theory – but it doesn't work well in practice. If the economy is operating below full capacity with balanced trade, there is no force operating to send the nominal exchange rate lower. On all the usual assumptions, in the usual neo-classical model, however, if the economy is operating below full capacity then the price and wage level should fall, thereby reducing the *real* exchange rate.

But we know the practical limitations to this. Except in extreme circumstances, price and wage levels are sticky downwards. Accordingly, it may be difficult, and at least take a very long time, for the required reduction in the real exchange rate to be delivered by domestic deflation.

Meanwhile, if effective controls are in place to limit capital outflows, or encourage inflows, then the real exchange rate does not need to fall. In other words, the term 'equilibrium' has to be interpreted accordingly to the policies in place at the time.

Can the exchange rate ever be too low?

If a country deliberately engineered a very low real exchange rate this would result in disturbances to its domestic economy. At first, inflationary pressure would be stronger and other policy settings would have to be tighter in order to prevent a low exchange rate (and a current account surplus) from causing continuing inflation.

Equally, there is an idea that a certain amount of pressure exerted on producers from a high and rising exchange rate is a good thing as it forces them to make productivity gains. To the extent that this is true, then having a much lower exchange rate will disincentivise firms from making such gains. (Strictly speaking, they would still have the incentive but they may not feel that effort in this direction is imperative.)

In practice, we suspect that there is a major difference between a 'high' and a 'rising' exchange rate. An exchange rate can be so high that it wipes out virtually all domestic production in certain sectors. At this point no stimulus to secure efficiency gains is felt. By contrast, if the exchange rate begins at a level competitive enough to enable a significant domestic presence in a range of activities, then a rising rate may well bring benefits of the sort described above. But the pace at which the exchange rate rises is vital. If the currency rises by 20-30% in a year – which has happened with the pound on more than one occasion – it is surely impossible for industries to make efficiency gains that offset this.

Nominal and real rates

Accordingly, if a fall in the real exchange rate is warranted there are often good reasons why this may not occur naturally. Equally, there are conditions when a fall in the nominal rate will succeed, and others when it will not succeed, in reducing the real rate. We need to examine these various conditions.

We can analyse when a depreciation of the nominal rate can be expected to achieve a sustained fall in the real rate and when it cannot. Essentially, the best chance to get and keep the real exchange rate low after a depreciation in the nominal rate occurs when there is slack in the domestic economy. In these conditions, it is possible to increase net exports and the overall level of GDP by utilising unemployed and under-employed resources of labour and capital.

By contrast, when the economy is fully employed, by definition it is impossible to increase GDP overall. Accordingly, if net exports are to increase, other components of aggregate demand have to be squeezed. So it is that devaluations have tended to work best in the context of recession.

When recessionary conditions do not exist, it is still possible for a devaluation to improve the trade balance, but only if domestic demand falls. Usually this requires the government deliberately to set out to squeeze domestic demand by raising taxes and/or cutting its own expenditure to 'make room' for an improvement in overseas trade. For understandable, largely political, reasons, governments are often loathe to squeeze demand hard enough, with the result that the devaluation disappoints, or perhaps even fails altogether.

Exchange rates in practice

So much for the theory. We also have considerable practical evidence on this matter. In the UK, the devaluation of 1967 had a major impact on markets' and policymakers' views and prejudices about exchange rate changes. The move was widely believed to have failed. It was certainly followed by higher inflation, eventually culminating in the inflationary blow-off of the mid-1970s. The result was that the gain to competitiveness was short-lived, as Figures 13 and 14 show.

So it was that when the UK again found itself in a fixed exchange rate system during its brief sojourn in the ERM

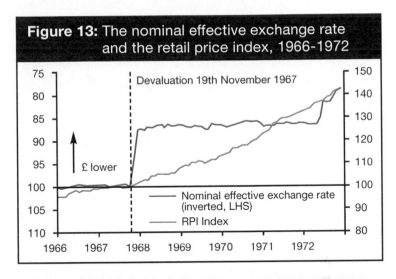

Figure 13: The nominal effective exchange rate and the retail price index, 1966-1972

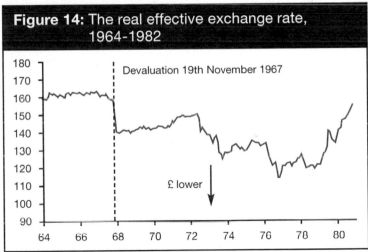

Figure 14: The real effective exchange rate, 1964-1982

from 1990-92, the Treasury view at the time was that we had to stay in the system because, if we chose to leave, the result would be higher inflation, which would necessitate higher interest rates, without creating any boost to net trade or GDP. In the event, as forecast by both of the present co-authors, when we did leave the ERM in September 1992, the result was exactly the opposite. Inflation fell, interest rates were cut, bond yields fell, and the economy embarked upon a sustained, and well-balanced recovery. And the real exchange rate stayed down – until the nominal rate rose again in 1996-7, as Figure 15 shows. (More about this later.)

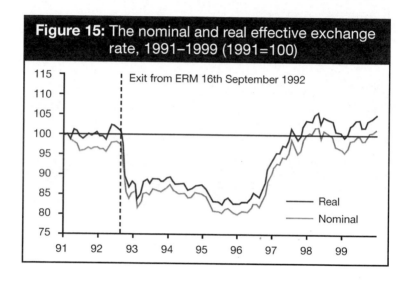

Figure 15: The nominal and real effective exchange rate, 1991–1999 (1991=100)

When thinking about the consequences of a lower exchange rate, the previous episode that the Treasury – and the markets – should have borne in mind in 1992 was not 1967 but 1931, when the UK left the gold standard. After 1931, the real exchange rate was significantly reduced and stayed down for several years. Admittedly, by 1938 the real rate was more or less back to where it had been in 1930, or even a bit higher. But this was not due mainly to higher domestic inflation. Rather, it was largely due to an appreciation of the nominal rate brought about by other countries devaluing (see Figure 16). Immediately after the break with Gold in 1931, the price level continued to fall. From 1934 onwards it was rising again but only modestly.

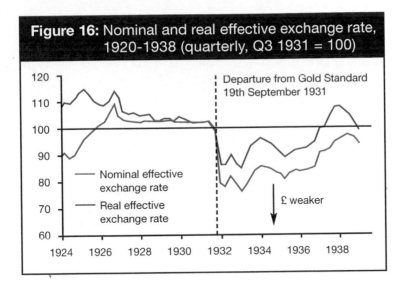

Figure 16: Nominal and real effective exchange rate, 1920-1938 (quarterly, Q3 1931 = 100)

A more recent failure?

It is widely believed that the sharp fall of sterling in 2008/9 was another case of devaluation failing to deliver the goods. During this period, the exchange rate fell by more than 25% (see Figure 17). Although the inflation rate did subsequently pick up, there was no price explosion so the real exchange rate stayed down. Again, although the real rate subsequently rose again quite sharply, this was mainly due to a rise in the nominal rate rather than to much higher domestic inflation (see Figures 17 and 18). Yet despite the early substantial fall in the real exchange rate, the current account barely budged. Indeed, in 2014 it was running at 5% of GDP, and in some periods reached 6%, a peacetime record.

So this was an episode that appeared to demonstrate, not that it was impossible to lower the real exchange rate by reducing the nominal rate, but rather that reductions in the real exchange rate don't seem to have much effect. On this occasion, it can hardly be said that this was because of an absence of spare capacity. Indeed, the financial crisis of 2008/9 caused GDP to plummet and unemployment to rise. Accordingly, many commentators have suggested that this period is evidence of the waning power of exchange rates to influence the trade balance, and hence the real economy.

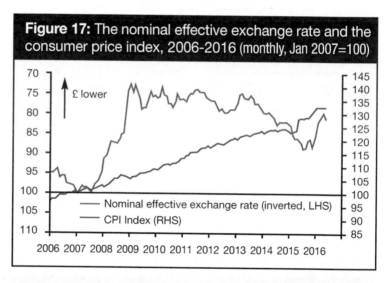

Figure 17: The nominal effective exchange rate and the consumer price index, 2006-2016 (monthly, Jan 2007=100)

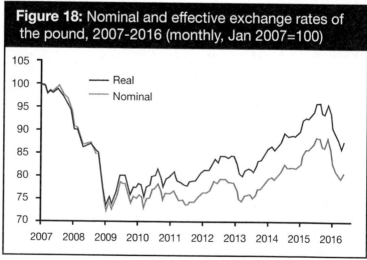

Figure 18: Nominal and effective exchange rates of the pound, 2007-2016 (monthly, Jan 2007=100)

In fact, this is not quite the conclusion that emerges from a careful interpretation of this episode. For a start, if you focus on the UK's trade balance rather than the overall current account, as shown in Figure 19, then there was some sign of improvement after the currency's sharp fall.

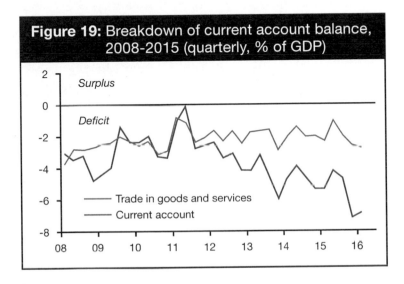

Figure 19: Breakdown of current account balance, 2008-2015 (quarterly, % of GDP)

Second, sterling fell sharply against the backdrop of a global recession, with our main markets on the continent particularly hard hit. These were not the conditions in which to expect a major improvement in the trade balance. If it did not deteriorate that may well have been evidence enough of a significant beneficial effect from the lower exchange rate.

Third, after the financial crisis, the banking system was in shut-down mode, with bank credit difficult to come by. In these circumstances businesses find expansion difficult, including expanding exports. Accordingly, exporting firms may well have reacted to the lower exchange rate by leaving foreign currency prices largely unchanged, thereby opting for higher profit margins over increased volumes. (This effect has been confirmed in a recent IMF study on exchange rate depreciation: 'Exchange Rates and Trade Flows: Disconnected?' in IMF, World Economic Outlook, Chapter 3, October 2015.)

Fourth, before very long the real exchange rate began to rise again, not because inflation took off (although for a time it was higher in the UK that in most advanced countries) but because the nominal rate started to climb. Not only did this retard the improvement in net trade but the perception that the reduction in the exchange rate might be temporary (and that it might even be resisted by the authorities) will have inhibited investment.

Brexit wobbles

In early 2016 the pound fell on fears that the UK might vote to leave the EU. After the vote it again fell sharply. It remains to be seen whether it falls further. But before this episode the pound was unhelpfully strong. On 18 June 2016, just a few days before the UK's EU referendum, held on 23 June, the IMF said that the pound was over-valued by 12-18%.

The true extent of the pounds over-valuation has often been obscured by movements of the pound against the dollar. A strong dollar means that sterling's exchange rate against that currency has recently been in territory that most of British industry finds reasonable. By contrast, in 2015/16 the pound's rate against the euro had climbed inexorably to the point that it was trading only some 10% below the peak reached before the 2007/8 financial crisis (see Figure 20). The euro is much more important for Britain's trade. The best way of measuring the pound's value is by reference to its trade-weighted index, often referred to as the 'effective exchange rate'. On this measure, by late 2015 the pound had given up more than 80% of the fall in its real exchange rate achieved in 2008/9.

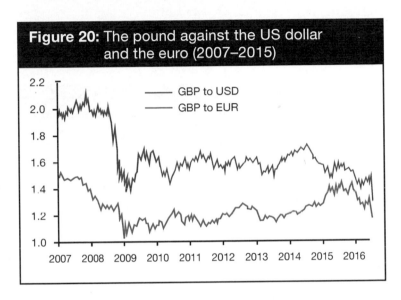

Figure 20: The pound against the US dollar and the euro (2007–2015)

Examples outside the UK

The relevance of conditions in the domestic economy when the currency is devalued is borne out by evidence from outside the UK. Countries that have a high initial degree of slack tend to be able to sustain a larger depreciation in the real exchange rate. This is the lesson of the experience of several countries shown in Figure 21. The experience of Argentina with the break of the peso's link with the dollar in 2001 is a clear example.

Argentina

Argentina abandoned its uncompetitive currency peg to the US dollar in early 2002, and the peso subsequently dropped by almost 70%. This caused substantial short-term pain for many creditors, households and firms, and led to widespread bankruptcies and bank failures. But by improving competitiveness at a stroke, it set the scene for a dramatic recovery. GDP growth averaged 9% per annum between 2003 and 2007, while employment rose by over 20% over this period (see Figure 22).

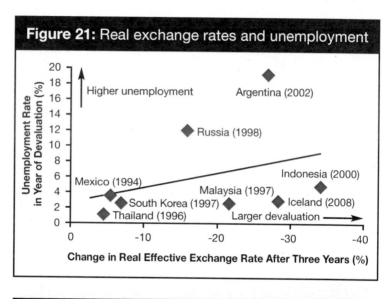

Figure 21: Real exchange rates and unemployment

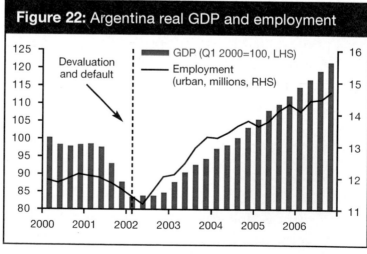

Figure 22: Argentina real GDP and employment

Crucially, Argentina was able to benefit from a more competitive currency because the weakness of the economy in the years prior to the devaluation had caused large amounts of spare capacity to open up. These underutilised resources could then be employed to raise output quickly as net exports picked up and lower real interest rates laid the foundations for a surge in investment.

Iceland

Iceland's healthy economic recovery after its financial collapse in 2008 also illustrates the potential attractions of currency depreciation. Between July 2007 and August 2009, Iceland's real effective exchange rate (adjusted for CPI) fell by over 40%. Admittedly, this caused inflation to surge to over 18% in late 2008. But inflation has since been tamed and GDP has risen in every year since 2010. A key driver of this recovery has been net trade, which between Q1 2008 and Q3 2015 made a very healthy contribution to Icelandic GDP to the tune of 16.5 percentage points (see Figures 23 and 24).

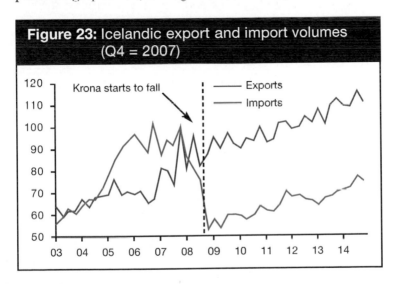

Figure 23: Icelandic export and import volumes (Q4 = 2007)

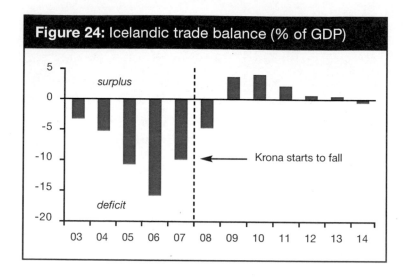

Figure 24: Icelandic trade balance (% of GDP)

Conclusion

There are circumstances when an economy needs a lower exchange rate. In these circumstances a depreciation of the nominal rate need not be fully offset by an upsurge of the price level. What's more, there are a number of instances when such a result, that is to say a depreciation of the real exchange rate, has been achieved, in both the UK and other countries.

There is ample evidence that before pre-Brexit worries and the drop of the pound after the Brexit vote brought the exchange rate to substantially lower levels, sterling was significantly over-valued. In these circumstances, there is no reason why the real exchange rate cannot be kept down – with enduring benefit to the economy.

The key worry in today's UK situation is surely not that an upsurge of inflation will cause the real exchange rate to return to where it began but rather that, as so often before, the nominal exchange rate will be allowed to climb yet again. That is where exchange rate policy comes in.

Part Three

Policy Proposals

8

Exchange rates and policy objectives

The policy issues raised in this pamphlet can be decomposed into two parts:

(i) If needed, how can the UK authorities get the exchange rate down?

(ii) How can policy be structured so as to keep it down?

In the right circumstances, a one-off fall of the pound could be achieved without the policy authorities doing anything at all. In early 2016, for instance, the pound fell sharply on fears that the UK would vote to leave the EU. After the Brexit vote, it fell further. In the wake of the financial crisis of 2008/9 the pound fell precipitately – by some 25% on average. On neither occasion did this arise from anything that the policy authorities said or did, or threatened or even intimated. The move occurred solely because the market changed its view of the fundamentals such that what now seemed to be the appropriate value for sterling was a good deal lower than it had been.

If the exchange rate is too high, it is better that an adjustment should occur 'naturally', because this avoids the distortions that might arise from deliberate policy actions and because this overcomes the difficulties, discussed below, posed by having to adhere to the G7's undertaking not to pursue exchange rate policies. Nevertheless, if the policy authorities wished to keep the pound at its new level they might have to resort to definite policy measures of the sort described in the next chapter.

If, in an ideal world, the pound could fall of its own accord, also in an ideal world it could keep at its low level without further manipulation of policy – whether its new level had been arrived at naturally, through market forces, or whether it had been nudged there through deliberate policy action.

This might seem fanciful but in fact it is more plausible than you might imagine. Once established at the 'right' level, markets might well perceive that the pound was appropriately valued and that departures from that range were unjustified. Across most of the industrialised world, central banks are aiming for roughly the same rate of inflation, namely 2% and in today's world it is unlikely that the UK's inflation rate will diverge markedly from the average of other countries. Once the exchange rate is at a competitive level, there is no reason why it should need to fall continually or repeatedly.

Nevertheless, often policy action will be required, either to get the pound lower to start with, to keep it lower, or both. Such policy action is discussed in the next chapter. But before that, there are some key issues concerning the theory of economic policy that need to be discussed.

Exchange rate management and inflation targets

Suppose that the government wanted to manage the exchange rate. What would that imply for the rate of inflation and its control? If the authorities set their sights on a lower exchange rate this would, for all the usual reasons, tend to raise the domestic price level – although, for the reasons spelled out elsewhere in this pamphlet, this tendency may not be acute and, in some cases, especially if assisted by a cut in indirect taxation, the price level could even fall. But where the price level is driven up there is no need for this to cause a continuing boost to the inflation rate. In the right circumstances, the inflation rate will flick up, reflecting the temporary boost to the price level, and then subside back to where it was in the first place.

But what are the right circumstances? Either the economy begins with a significant margin of under-used resources (under-employment) or if it doesn't then other components of aggregate demand fall back (perhaps induced by policy) to make room for the increase in demand from abroad brought about by the lower exchange rate.

But after this one-off result, how would an exchange rate target interact with anti-inflation policy? In many circumstances this would not be a problem. If the inflation rate in other countries were broadly the same as the inflation objective in this country – and at the moment just about all countries seem to be aiming at something close to 2% - then exchange rate fixity could deliver a reasonable basis for meeting our own inflation objective. (This was evidently believed by the UK Treasury during the period in the late 1980s when the authorities covertly operated a policy of shadowing the Deutschemark.) One can think of a number of circumstances, however, in which a clash could occur:-

(i) A sharp rise in import prices, perhaps driven by oil and commodity prices causes the domestic price level to rise. If domestic interest rates were being used to maintain the exchange rate, they could not be raised in these circumstances to suppress inflation.

(ii) For whatever reason, UK domestic demand surges, requiring some form of restraint to prevent inflation from rising.

(iii) For whatever reason, there is a surge in UK exports and given the state of domestic demand, this threatens higher inflation.

In practice, case (i) is less of a problem than it may appear. Under the present regime of inflation targeting the Bank of England (along with other central banks) has in the recent past 'looked through' such temporary spikes in the inflation rate and did not move interest rates in response. There need be no difference under a policy regime that gave weight to the exchange rate.

Both cases (ii) and (iii), however, are very different in an exchange rate targeting world. Under an inflation target, in both cases interest rates would be raised to squeeze demand. This is precisely what cannot easily be done in an exchange rate management world, without recourse to other policy instruments, about which more in a moment. Mind you, if higher inflation is allowed to result this need not be permanent in that the higher inflation would itself, with the given nominal exchange rate target adhered to, cause a rise in the real exchange rate, which would cause a deterioration in the net trade balance which would reduce aggregate demand and thereby stop the forces making for accelerating inflation.

Even so, this is far from being a panacea. It would be more appropriate in case (iii) in that, ex hypothesi, what sets off the inflationary danger is an incipient improvement in the trade balance. Accordingly, it is not inappropriate that this is reversed by a rise in the real exchange rate that brings the trade balance back to where it was in the first place.

In case (ii), however, the result would be relying on a deterioration in the external account to offset a surge in domestic demand, which is hardly in accordance with the objective of having an exchange rate target in the first place, namely to ensure a healthy trade balance. Moreover, once a higher rate of inflation has been established, it might well become ingrained (expected), with all the usual welfare costs, even after the real exchange rate had risen sufficiently to choke off enough aggregate demand to stabilise the exchange rate.

Furthermore, with a higher rate of inflation in place, the nominal exchange rate would have to be regularly shifted down in order to maintain the real exchange rate at the target level.

More instruments to meet more targets

It is widely accepted that the authorities need to have at least as many policy instruments as there are objectives. It is frequently argued that this means that, given that we have an inflation target, central banks cannot simultaneously pursue an exchange rate policy. Implicitly, the assumption is that the authorities have only one instrument, namely the official short term interest rate, and that is set in order to hit the inflation target.

In fact, the problem applies more generally than just in relation to the exchange rate. Indeed, in most countries the central bank has not one objective but two, namely, not only to achieve a specified inflation objective, but also to achieve objectives for the real economy, defined as a mixture of growth and employment. In the US this other objective has equal weight to the inflation objective; in the UK, the growth and employment objective is subsidiary. In neither country, however, has it been made explicitly clear how the central bank is to pursue these two objectives simultaneously.

We discuss what extra instruments might be available to meet extra policy objectives in the next chapter.

Doing without an inflation target

One option, of course, is to do without an inflation target altogether. Provided that conditions in the world are fairly stable and the overall inflation rate is low this is not such a daft option as it might seem. After all, it would represent a return to pretty much the regime that operated in most countries before the advent of inflation targets. Indeed, under the Bretton Woods system, every country except the United States relied on the fixed exchange rate to provide an anchor for nominal values. But this system depended, of course, on the United States pursuing something like price stability itself. If it didn't, then the fixed exchange rate system would ensure that price instability was transmitted around the world.

Meanwhile, the option of deploying a Keynesian expansion in the event of a major shortfall of aggregate demand – and indeed dropping interest rates and even reducing the exchange rate target – would still be there. Again, though, operating policy according to an explicit exchange rate target would run counter to our G7 undertakings which we discuss later.

What other countries do

Although we like to think that we live in a world of floating currencies, in fact a substantial number of the world's economies operate an exchange rate policy, or rather policies. There is a considerable range.

At one extreme is the currency peg operated by Hong Kong. Although it issues its own currency – the Hong Kong dollar – not only is the rate of exchange between the HK$ and the US$ fixed by the HK authorities but the country operates a currency board system under which changes in the domestic money supply (the monetary base) exactly correspond to inflows and outflows of US dollars. To all intents and purposes under this system the Hong Kong authorities have given up all independence of monetary policy. Hong Kong is effectively a full part of the US dollar zone. Hong Kong dollars are a mere token; they are US dollars in disguise.

At the other extreme is Singapore's exchange rate policy. This is not a fixed rate of exchange; rather the authorities seek to manage the Singapore dollar against a basket of other currencies within a pre-determined range. But Singapore does not have an inflation target. Accordingly, the inflation rate does fluctuate considerably, with drops into deflation, alternating with bursts of inflation.

Conflict with inflation targeting?

There are many ways to skin a cat. It would be possible for the exchange rate to play a greater role in economic policy without it necessarily figuring prominently in the objectives of economic policy. Nevertheless, without some formal acknowledgement, there is a risk that it would continue to be some flabbily acknowledged other factor lurking in the background, while prominence was given to other variables. If the exchange rate really is that important, then surely it should figure more prominently in policy objectives, just as it has done in the case of so many other countries throughout the world, as discussed in the previous chapter. Moreover, if the exchange rate does not figure as a policy objective it is difficult for domestic producers to be confident that their competitive position will not soon be undermined by a surge in the exchange rate.

Over recent decades, the idea of putting exchange rates in a prominent position has conflicted with the widespread adherence to inflation targets. And with effective policy instruments thin on the ground, this has severely constrained the authorities from pursuing other objectives.

Yet surely we can all acknowledge that the inflation targeting regime is due for improvement. It came into existence after a period when inflation was rampant and threatened to destabilise the whole capitalist system. This time has long passed. More or less everywhere, inflation is low to non-existent – or even negative. Moreover, if it ends up being plus or minus one, two or three per cent, so what? The notion that central banks should devote every effort to fine-tuning the supposedly likely outcome of inflation in two or three years' time is for the birds. They used not to behave this way and they should not be doing so now.

Nevertheless, there would still have to be some sort of nominal anchor, as there was under both the gold standard and the Bretton Woods system. We discuss what that might be below. It should be possible to fashion a regime in which objectives for the exchange rate sit easily with inflation targets. In short, although they are not the be-all and end-all of economic policy, we need inflation targets – as well as a policy of exchange rate management.

An exchange rate target?

As far as exchange rate management is concerned, it is widely assumed that the natural alternative to total neglect is complete fixity, or at least single-minded targeting of a level or range for the exchange rate. But this need not be so. The important thing is that the policy authorities should have a clear idea, announced in public and communicated to the markets, of what the exchange rate should reasonably be. If it veers outside this range, then there should be a presumption that something is wrong and perhaps policy needs to be adjusted accordingly.

This can be compared with the situation facing the Federal Reserve in the United States. It has a dual mandate – to achieve both price stability and full employment. And it effectively only has one policy instrument, namely the short term official interest rate.

The role of an explicit statement about the exchange rate is threefold: first, to influence the expectations of market participants; second, to constrain and influence government policy with regard to both interest rates and the fiscal balance – as well as other factors that influence the attractiveness of UK assets; third, to give confidence to firms that they can invest and plan for the future on the back of a competitive exchange rate.

9

How to get the exchange rate lower

Suppose that the authorities decide that the exchange rate should be lower. What could they do to bring this about? Possible policies fall into five broad types:

(i) Changes to the macroeconomic policy mix, e.g. running a tighter fiscal policy in order to make a possible looser monetary policy (i.e. lower interest rates and/or more quantitative easing (QE) than otherwise);

(ii) Prudential policy tools, including reserve requirements and capital requirements;

(iii) Intervention on the foreign exchanges;

(iv) Talk and guidance, perhaps even extending to the publication of targets;

(v) Micro policies designed to make UK assets less attractive to overseas investors.

In principle, of course, it would also be possible to deploy capital controls, and many countries do – including China. But capital controls are distortionary, as well as being against our undertakings to both the EU and the G7. They don't have any practical appeal for a country like the UK. Accordingly, we do not include them in the list of five types of instrument, described above.

1. The Macroeconomic Policy Mix

In principle, fiscal policy could provide the extra policy instrument. In theory it would be possible to use changes in fiscal policy to constrain the growth of aggregate demand to the growth of productive capacity and therefore forestall and/or correct a movement of inflation away from the target.

In practice, though, fiscal fine tuning is not a viable proposition. It is not economically desirable or politically attractive to make short-term adjustments to the fiscal balance, through either tax changes or changes to planned expenditure. Nor do short-term fiscal adjustments have predictable effects on aggregate demand. Nevertheless, it is a viable proposition to set fiscal policy on a course that would facilitate the maintenance of a competitive exchange rate.

Running a tight fiscal policy would certainly help to establish and sustain a policy of low interest rates without necessarily landing the country with an inflation problem. But it does not really constitute a second policy instrument that would allow the authorities to pursue two policy objectives. Firstly, in most countries, including the UK, fiscal policy is set with regard to another objective, namely reducing the ratio of government debt to GDP on a path that is deemed optimal, balancing the need to reduce the total, and retain bond market confidence, against the need to avoid delivering a shock to aggregate demand through tightening too quickly.

In the UK there has been a fervent debate about the appropriate degree of fiscal tightening, with critics of the government arguing that it is planning to tighten too much. But in this debate scant regard has been paid to the exchange rate. It deserves much more attention.

Some of the criticism of the government's fiscal stance derives from the idea that there is considerable spare capacity in the economy and that the tight fiscal policy thereby leads to unnecessary waste of resources. This may or may not be true but what matters for policy is what the Bank of England believes.

If the Bank believes that there is no margin of unused capacity then, if fiscal policy were to be looser, the Bank would set interest rates above where they would otherwise have been. Other things equal, that would tend to increase the exchange rate for sterling, with the usual adverse consequences for our competitiveness and hence for the current account.

Even without the assumption of unused resources, of course, the critics of current fiscal policy may have a point with regard to with the unfair/unjust/unnecessary/inefficient squeeze on the public sector relative to what is going on in the private sector. In particular, they could point to the squeeze on public investment.

But without the unused resources assumption they should surely take account of the potential damage to our current account that a looser fiscal policy would imply, recognising that a larger current account deficit would imply a worsened national wealth position which would offset at least some of the gain from higher public investment.

So what role can fiscal policy play with regard to management of the UK exchange rate? Taking it as a given that the position of public investment should be protected, concern to improve the current account position argues for a tighter fiscal stance. In ordinary conditions this would be demanding enough politically and it is so now. But in current circumstances at least tighter policy fits in with the objective of reducing the ratio of government debt to GDP. Operating a tighter policy would result in a lower ratio being achieved, or the same ratio being achieved sooner.

In this regard, it is important to recognise a potential change in circumstances. When interest rates were at rock bottom (and the authorities appear to have regarded 0.5% as rock bottom for the UK) and there were doubts about the wisdom and/or effectiveness of more QE, a tighter fiscal policy would not have delivered looser monetary policy, and therefore would not have helped to sustain a weaker exchange rate. These have been the conditions for the last several years.

Very low rates are now likely to continue for an extended period. But thereafter we will enter a period when interest rates are set to rise. In these circumstances, a tighter fiscal policy could put back a rise in rates, and continue to keep rates lower than they would have been under the original fiscal policy. They could also justify more QE, whether this is conducted across the exchanges (foreign exchange intervention) or not. (See below.)

2. Prudential policy tools

In practice, in the UK there has over recent years been some amelioration of potential policy conflict through the development of a prudential policy toolkit. This has assuredly not been developed in order to allow policy to pay explicit regard to the exchange rate but rather to allow the central bank to pursue objectives for both the inflation rate and financial stability.

In principle, this extra set of tools would be available to help manage the exchange rate. For instance, suppose that a burgeoning inflation problem seemed to require higher interest rates to head it off; it might be possible to address this by deploying a tightening of prudential policy without requiring higher interest rates, which might threaten to send the pound higher on the exchanges.

But, of course, if prudential policy is there to address concerns of financial stability, it cannot be used simultaneously, except by happy coincidence, to help manage the exchange rate. So another instrument is needed.

3. Foreign exchange intervention

Foreign exchange intervention has acquired a bad name – along with the policy of exchange rate management. There are good reasons for this. Usually, intervention has been employed to stop a currency from falling. This involves selling foreign currency and buying domestic currency.

This has a clear limitation. The domestic monetary authorities can run out of supplies of foreign currency to sell (the foreign exchange reserves) and their access to further supplies through borrowing will also be limited.

There are countless examples of countries finding it impossible to hold the exchange rate up against apparently limitless waves of selling. Perhaps the best example is when the Bank of England tried and failed to keep the pound in the European Exchange Rate Mechanism (ERM) in September 1992.

But the position is different when central banks are trying to keep their currencies down. In this case they have to sell domestic currency and buy foreign currency.

In principle, there is no limit to the amount of domestic currency that they can issue – and therefore no limit to the amount that they can sell.

In practice, though, there is a limit of sorts. Issuing more domestic currency inflates the money supply and if this is continued without offsetting policies then it threatens to cause an upsurge of inflation.

The obvious offsetting policy is to sell extra domestic assets to absorb the inflow of money. This is the policy known as sterilisation. In principle, this can continue without limit but it too has complications. A central bank has a limited range of assets that it can sell in order to absorb currency inflows – usually some sort of fixed interest instruments such as bonds or quasi-deposits. But money pouring in from abroad may seek employment in a whole panoply of assets, including not only bonds and bank deposits but also residential and commercial property and equities. In that case, selling large amounts of bonds and quasi-deposit type instruments may cause distortions in financial markets.

There is also the issue of the profitability of the central bank intervention. This can limit the extent of the gains from the policy – and certainly curtail central banks' appetite for pursuing it. The effect on profitability depends, as usual, on two elements: capital gains and income.

If the central bank sells domestic currency to acquire foreign currency assets and is eventually obliged to let the currency rise then it will incur a capital loss.

The income element depends upon the relative cost of the domestic currency bonds that the central bank has to issue to raise the money to sell on the exchanges versus the interest income that can be earned on foreign currency assets. As it happens, in current circumstances, the UK government can borrow at very low interest rates.

The clearest example of a country finding it next to impossible to hold the exchange rate down is Switzerland in 2015. The Swiss National Bank tried to hold the Swiss franc down by dint of huge sales of Swiss francs on the exchanges. But in January 2015 it decided that it could hold on no longer and let the currency rise. This episode supposedly revealed that foreign exchange intervention is ultimately ineffective, even when the central bank is selling (and issuing) its own currency.

But the Swiss case is potentially highly misleading. In 2015, Switzerland ran a current account surplus of 11.4% of GDP, roughly 1.6 times the surplus (proportionately) of Germany, and 3.8 times that of China. The scale of this surplus indicated that without a radical change of circumstances or policy, the Swiss franc was substantially under-valued. Accordingly, it is no wonder that the Swiss National Bank could not hold the currency down.

There are also some clear examples of countries imposing substantial and painful distortions on their economies by operating policies that kept their exchange rates artificially low with the result that they ran substantial current account surpluses, whilst reducing consumption below what it could otherwise be. China and Japan fall into this category and so, arguably, does Germany. These examples do not set a happy precedent for the UK.

Needless to say, however, the UK is in a very different position. It has been running a huge current account deficit and there has been clear evidence that the currency has been over-valued. Accordingly, intervention to hold it down would be working with the grain of the economic fundamentals, not against them.

Quantitative easing could be deployed across the exchanges, that is to say, the Bank of England could purchase overseas assets. (This is good old fashioned intervention in the foreign exchange market.)

Perhaps this could even be done via the establishment of a UK sovereign wealth fund. Suppose that a country establishes a funded pension scheme by means of enforced deductions from pay. The funds received need to be invested somewhere. As with private schemes, it would be normal (and good) practice to invest a proportion of these funds abroad. The smaller the country in question, other things equal, the greater should be the proportion invested abroad. This may or may not result in downward pressure on the exchange rate, depending upon the response of individuals to the deductions from their pay (lower saving or lower spending) and the balance of domestic versus overseas in whatever individuals' responses are.

In current circumstances, it would be impossible to raise extra money through taxation, and/or enforce deductions from pay (over and above those already in train under the government's new pension policy). Might it be possible to establish such a fund by borrowing? The UK government could establish an overseas investment fund, with money invested in overseas securities, funded by the issue of gilts. This would definitely exert downward pressure on the exchange rate. It would be the equivalent of a policy of QE but with foreign rather than domestic assets purchased.

A more discreet way of achieving the same thing would be to establish a fund to receive existing national insurance contributions, or at least a fraction of them, to be invested abroad. Of course the funds thus channelled into overseas investment would not be available for ordinary domestic expenditure and this would therefore create a domestic financial shortfall, which would have to be covered by borrowing. Accordingly, it amounts to the same idea as the one discussed above. But it may be presentationally and practically attractive, including in the way that it is presented to our G7 partners.

Under this suggestion, the official figures for net borrowing would be unaltered since extra gross borrowing would be offset by asset purchases. This would be the equivalent of a bout of ordinary sterilised foreign exchange intervention. To make this equivalent to unsterilised intervention the Bank of England would buy gilts equivalent to the extra ones issued. This would produce a situation akin to ordinary QE, except that there would now be extra gilts in issue, mirroring (and financing) the foreign securities held by the new Sovereign (Pension/National Insurance) fund.

4. Verbal direction and encouragement

Talk and guidance might seem attractive since this may be thought to have the smallest cost in regard to the distortion of policies in order to achieve an exchange rate objective. But unless it is backed up by one or more of the other policy instruments it is also unlikely to be very effective. Moreover, it is the policy lever that most obviously conflicts with our G7 obligations.

Equally, unless there is some verbal articulation of a new exchange rate policy, deployment of each of the other instruments may not be as effective as it might be since businesses might not perceive the change of policy and therefore might not fully believe that whatever exchange rate change happens is going to last. So ideally a policy to reduce the pound and or to keep it at its new lower level would involve a combination of all of the above instruments – and the perception that the authorities potentially have more of the same up their sleeve to deploy if necessary.

The power of words should not be under-estimated, particularly with regard to keeping a currency down, given that such words are backed up by the full panoply of macro and micro policy. Even if they stop short of declaring a formal range within which they intend the pound to trade (which would be against current G7 rules), the UK policy authorities could make it clear that they aim to keep the exchange rate competitive and that this objective will occupy a central place in their policy deliberations and policy settings.

5. Micro policies designed to make UK assets less attractive

(i) A different policy on foreign acquisition of UK companies

Most countries are wary of allowing overseas interests to own and control more than a limited proportion of their major companies for strategic or other reasons. By both formal and informal methods, making unwanted take-overs difficult to accomplish, they have ways of discouraging overseas acquisition of businesses which they think are of national significance. In 2005, the French government drafted a law to protect 'strategic industries' from being purchased by companies owned elsewhere, thus protecting Danone, best known for its yoghurts, from being purchased by Pepsi-Cola or Nestle. In the same year, the US Senate passed a bill blocking the purchase of a number of US ports by Dubai Ports World on the grounds that this might compromise US security.

In the UK, the old Monopolies and Mergers Commission was able to apply a public interest test to takeover proposals and the UK was therefore able to behave in a similar way to most other countries.

This changed in 1999, however, when the Monopolies and Mergers Commission was replaced by the Competition Commission which had no such remit. In the then prevailing UK climate of opinion – the market knows best and who owns or controls UK companies does not matter as long as competition is not impaired – the Competition Commission had no role to play in taking a view as to whether UK companies being acquired by overseas interests might have a wider national significance. As a result, the UK – encouraged by the City, which made large sums from the fees involved – became a happy hunting ground for any international company wanting to expand its foreign interests.

While direct investment in plant and machinery from foreign-owned business tends to be strongly advantageous to the UK economy, the overseas purchasing and ownership of existing companies has none of these advantages. It also has major downsides. Control goes abroad, and with it are inclined to go key research and investment decisions. Much of the tax base of such companies also goes abroad – certainly corporate tax. Also, often, the tax of non-dom executives. For entirely understandable reasons, international companies are bound to have a special regard for their home markets. With ownership goes the flow of profits and capital gains.

For all these reasons, a first step to take would be to reintroduce a public interest test for all takeovers, particularly those involving ownership and control from abroad, with these tests designed to take the wider interests of the UK economy as a whole into account, and not just narrow issues about competition.

The sums involved in allowing complete freedom for overseas takeovers are significant. In 2015, total overseas participation in the acquisition of UK companies amounted to just over £30bn. This compares to an overall current account deficit of £100bn. Between 2000 and 2007 the average annual inflow was £44bn. (Of course, we need to bear in mind that the UK is also highly active in purchasing companies overseas.)

(ii) Foreign acquisition of UK property

Net sales of UK property assets on a major scale have stemmed from a different source. The UK in general and London in particular provide a safe and secure environment for those in less stable parts of the world. Purchasing properties in the UK has increasingly become an attractive – and prestigious - way of investing footloose funds which might otherwise be at risk. Especially recently, the scale on which residential property is being bought by overseas residents rather than UK residents is staggering. A recent report indicated that about 75% of all new build houses and flats in London were being bought by overseas residents, while about half of all property transactions in London of more than £1m again involved overseas purchasers. (Admittedly, this total includes UK purchasers using foreign/offshore corporate structures.)

The result of this huge external demand on top of a faltering supply, combined with the UK's rapidly rising population and very low interest rates for those in a position to borrow, has been a very rapid increase in house prices, freezing many potential first time buyers out of the market.

It is difficult to get hard and fast aggregate figures on the extent of overseas purchases of UK property. We estimate that since 2008, overseas companies and individuals may have bought about £150bn of UK commercial property and have sold about £90bn worth. So, in net terms, overseas asset purchases have amounted to about £60bn, some 17% of the value of all UK commercial property transactions over this period.

Data on residential sales are even sketchier. From the reports of leading estate agents it seems as though, between 2008 and mid-2014, about 10% of central London residential sales were to overseas buyers. On reasonable assumptions that would translate to a total inflow of just over £20bn.

As regards purchases of residential property, again there are fairly obvious routes to containing the scale on which this currently occurs. There could be much heavier taxation of foreign-owned houses and flats, especially those with very high value, where much of the problem resides. As most of the properties concerned are at the expensive end of the market, major tax increases focused on those owned by foreign registered companies or individuals domiciled abroad would only affect a limited number of housing units. This would be a further development of the policies already deployed by HM Treasury. But these have been pretty crudely designed to raise revenue and/or slow the top end of the market, rather than to target specifically the foreign purchase of UK property. (Interestingly, Australia prohibits foreigners from buying existing property but not from adding to the housing stock.)

Policies along these lines would not only reduce the upward pressure on the exchange rate, but they would also ease the strain on the UK property market generally, allowing more resources to be devoted to satisfying the housing needs of the indigenous population.

Conclusions on micro policy

We don't need to lift up the drawbridge and to isolate ourselves from world capital markets, but equally we do not need to have most of our ports, airports, large manufacturing companies, utilities, energy companies, rail franchises, football clubs and much of our housing and real estate in foreign ownership. We need a reasonable balance, in the same way that applies in almost all other countries.

Nor would such a policy necessarily be to the disadvantage of the rest of the world, broadly considered. When Russian capital flows out of Russia and into UK assets, real and financial, whatever this might do to the prosperity of individual Russian wealth-holders, is it really in the interests of Russia?

Admittedly, in normal circumstances, it would not make sense to use micro measures, such as restrictions on overseas investments in UK assets, as a substitute for macro measures in order to achieve macro objectives. But it makes sense to temper the overseas appetite for our real assets for soundly-based other reasons. The fact that such action would tend to weaken the forces that put upward pressure on our exchange rate is an added bonus.

The policy regime

The policy instruments discussed above are of very different sorts. The tightness of fiscal policy and the attractions of UK assets to overseas wealth holders are not things that can be deployed at a moment's notice to manage or influence the exchange rate. Rather, the settings of these variables can be made in regard to their impact on the exchange rate and then left there for extended periods. For short-term influence, the authorities would need to rely on extensive foreign exchange intervention, perhaps backed up by verbal guidance.

Equally, on their own, these two may not be very effective if they are deployed to try to achieve and sustain an exchange rate out of line with the economic fundamentals and with the stance of fiscal and monetary policy, and the relative attractiveness of UK assets to foreigners. What is needed is a policy regime which includes all these facets.

10

Objections to a lower exchange rate policy – and the answers

1. Currency devaluation (or depreciation) inevitably leads to higher inflation.

There are many examples of countries experiencing currency depreciation and rapid inflation interacting with each other, indeed, feeding off each other. These examples, usually involving developing countries, often burdened by weak and ineffectual governments, have been widely assumed to reveal a general truth about the linkages between the currency and the price level. They do not. In fact, for developed countries they can be extremely misleading.

It is true that even for developed countries, following currency depreciation, the price of imports is bound to rise. Indeed, this is a necessary part of switching demand from international to domestic suppliers. It does not follow, however, that the overall price level generally will rise more quickly than it would have done without a devaluation. A wealth of evidence from the dozens of devaluations and depreciations which have occurred among relatively rich and diversified economies such as ours in recent decades shows that in fact, although lower exchange rates usually lead to a rise in the price level, sometimes they produce a bit of a reduction, and sometimes little if any change compared to what would have occurred anyway.

Moreover, even when the price level does increase, so that the measured rate of inflation rises, at least for a time, generally the increase in inflation is short-lived. After the once-and-for-all price shock has passed through the system, the inflation rate may readily fall back to roughly where it was to begin with.

One of the clearest examples is when the UK left the Exchange Rate Mechanism in 1992. Sterling fell by a trade-weighted 17%, but inflation fell from 3.2% in August 1992 to 1.5% in September 1994.

The reason why inflation may not pick up much, if at all, is that, while higher import prices push up the price level, many factors to do with a lower exchange rate tend to bring it down. Interest rates tend to be lower and production runs become longer, bringing down average costs. Investment, especially in the most productive parts of the economy may rise, increasing output per head, reducing costs and producing a wage climate more conducive to keeping income increases in line with productivity growth.

2. In today's economy it is impossible to change the exchange rate.

It is frequently contended that the parity of sterling is determined by market forces over which the authorities have little control, so that any policy to change the exchange rate in any direction is bound to fail. Again, historical experience indicates that this proposition cannot be correct. The Japanese, to provide a recent example, brought the parity of the yen down by 10% between April 2013 and October 2014 as a result of deliberate policy (although the yen has since rebounded, partly because of safe haven demand). Further back, the Plaza Accord, negotiated in 1985, produced a massive change in parities among the major trading nations of the world at the time, causing the dollar to fall against the yen by 40% in the two years following the agreement.

Of course, market forces determine exchange rates but the authorities can influence the factors which determine what market forces are. If the UK pursues policies which make it very easy for overseas interests to buy British assets, for example, this will exert upward pressure on sterling's exchange rate. If the markets think that the Bank of England is going to raise interest rates, this will also push sterling higher.

Nor is it true that it is impossible to change the real exchange rate by altering the nominal rate. This is the perspective that whatever gain is achieved by a lower exchange rate is soon offset by a higher domestic price level. Accordingly, it is addressed by the remarks under 1 above.

3. Any benefit from depreciation would be lost through retaliation.
There is no doubt that this is a significant issue. Yet the eurozone has been able to benefit from a huge depreciation of the euro without suffering retaliation. And the UK, of course, is much less important in world trade than the eurozone.

Moreover, the case for retaliation depends, in part, on the position from which the devaluing country starts. The problem of overseas payments imbalances starts, not with countries like the UK, with massive deficits, but with economies such as Germany and Switzerland with huge surpluses – in 2014 running at about 8% of

GDP in Germany's case and 7% for Switzerland. These surpluses have to be matched by deficits somewhere else in the world economy.

Unfortunately, surplus countries are never under any immediate pressure to reduce the beggar-thy-neighbour impact of their surpluses by revaluing their currencies and this leaves economies such as ours, carrying big deficits, with no alternative but devaluation to get the situation under control. There is thus a very strong, principled case for countries such as the UK to make.

Actually, the boot should be on the other foot. It is not that the UK would encounter retaliation if she took action to reduce her exchange rate but rather that she is the sufferer from other countries' competitive depreciations, principally the eurozone's. It is the UK that needs to respond in order to preserve her own position. After the Brexit-inspired fall of the pound, the necessary response may simply amount to maintaining the new, competitive value for the pound.

4. Devaluation must make us all poorer.

Since import prices rise, depreciations tend to reduce the real incomes and living standards of many people. But this is not the end of the story. If a depreciation produces higher GDP then GDP per head will rise. Many people who did not have jobs will now have them and thus average incomes will rise. It is true that, for the depreciation to benefit the trade balance, there has to be an increase in net exports. While this will generate increased income it will not, directly, generate increased consumption. That is, after all, the point. Net exports represent consumption foregone.

Nevertheless, average living standards could rise if the increase in GDP, brought about by the depreciation, exceeds the increase in net exports plus any deterioration in the terms of trade (the ratio of export prices to import prices) and any redistribution of real income from workers to employers.

Many people assume that the terms of trade must deteriorate after a depreciation. They think this way because they reason that the depreciation 'raises the price of imports but reduces the price of exports'. Indeed, this change in relative prices, they reason, is the channel through which the depreciation is supposed to improve the trade balance.

But when they reason this way they are thinking in different currencies for imports and exports. This is misleading. If you think in the same currency for both exports and imports then you can readily see that a deterioration in the terms of trade is not inevitable.

Let us assume that we are dealing with a small country that cannot influence the world price of its imports and exports. Then a depreciation will have no effect on the foreign currency price of its imports and exports and the domestic price of both will rise by the full percentage of the depreciation, leaving the ratio of export to import prices unchanged. Whether a depreciation improves or worsens the terms of trade depends upon the relative monopoly/monopsony power of the country in the various markets in which it trades.

When Britain devalued the pound in 1967, the then Prime Minister, Harold Wilson, told the British public that 'the pound in your pocket has not been devalued'. The idea was that their purchasing power would not be reduced by the devaluation, or at least, not to the full extent. This statement was partly true – and partly highly misleading. At the very least, as import prices rose, other things equal, people's real incomes would fall. In the extreme, if there were no excess capacity then prices would rise beyond the increase in import prices.

In the end, the major determinants of whether people on average will be better or worse off in regard to their level of consumption as a result of devaluation will be: the extent of excess capacity; the extent of the need to cut back consumption in order to boost exports; the size of any deterioration in the terms of trade; and the size of any swing against real wages and towards real profits.

5. Past devaluations have not worked.

This is not true. Some devaluations that have taken place in the past have been too little and too late and have not worked. They might have made the situation better than it otherwise would have been but they have not transformed matters. The UK's devaluation of 1967 falls into this category. But some drops of the exchange rate have had a powerful effect – notably in 1931 and 1992.

Moreover, there are plenty of examples from other countries of depreciations having a major beneficial effect. Furthermore, umpteen countries around the world carefully manage their exchange rates precisely because they know that their exchange rates have a major bearing on their trade performance, and hence on their GDP.

6. The UK has no bent for manufacturing.

While it is true that a wide swathe of low- and medium-tech manufacturing is uneconomic in the UK at present, because the exchange rate and the cost base for them are much too high, there is no evidence whatever that if more favourable conditions prevailed, UK entrepreneurs would not be just as good as those anywhere else in the world at taking advantage of the new opportunities which would then open up. There is no evidence that the UK lacks entrepreneurial people who would be willing to try their hands at making money out of making and selling if the right opportunities were there. The problem with the UK as a manufacturing environment is that these conditions simply do not exist at the moment, because the cost base is too high, and entrepreneurs rightly shun investing in ventures which they can see from the beginning have poor prospects of being profitable and successful.

It is true that it is normal for rich and successful countries like the UK to experience a fall in the share of GDP accounted for by manufacturing. But this is not the be-all and end-all. Germany is at roughly the same level of development as the UK but its share of manufacturing is roughly twice the UK's. In part this reflects the different experience of the exchange rate of the two countries. Although Germany's nominal exchange rate, under the Deutschemark, tended to rise over time, it hardly ever experienced the sharp rises of the real exchange rate that UK manufacturers have suffered several times. And after the advent of the euro, Germany's real exchange rate has been kept low.

7. We should leave the exchange rate to be determined by market forces.

Market forces do not exist in a vacuum. They respond, in part, to the policy settings, macro and micro, imposed by the authorities.

To the extent that the UK exchange rate is sustained by overseas wealth holders' preferences for UK assets, it could be argued that this is just a particular manifestation of the 'market forces' to which the UK at present submits – and should do so. Yet the interests of foreign asset holders are not naturally congruent with the interests of UK citizens. The UK 'provides' some intangible things that overseas wealth holders value – political stability, the rule of law, liquidity. Other things being equal, the UK should be able to charge a fee for providing these things. It is frequently argued that this is just what the United States does in that it is able to borrow more cheaply than it otherwise would without having the 'exorbitant privilege' of issuing the world's money. To a lesser extent this should also be true of the UK.

But where is the comparable 'fee' secured by selling real assets to overseas wealth holders? And what if the attractions of UK (or US) assets to foreigners have the result of increasing the amount that needs to be financed? After all, if foreign capital inflows drive up the exchange rate and thereby induce an increased current account deficit then both the public sector (thanks to lower tax revenues) and the private sector (thanks to reduced incomes from net exports) will have to borrow more. In these circumstances it seems as though it is the host country that ends up paying a fee to attract overseas capital.

The key issue here is what the capital drawn into a country actually finances. If it is productive investment then that will bring a return that may offset – and more than offset – the cost. But if it merely finances consumption this will not be true. Worse than this, it will diminish total national income by pushing up the exchange rate. If we assume that other components of macroeconomic policy (interest rates, QE, tax policy) take up the slack so as to maintain full employment, then the overall loss of income will be avoided but it will remain the case that total national investment will have been reduced, and the overall national wealth diminished compared to what it would otherwise have been. This hardly seems to be to our national advantage.

Of course, it is not easy to tell the ultimate use to which a capital inflow is put. It is possible, for instance, that when an overseas company buys real assets – perhaps an existing UK company – from its current owners that the proceeds are invested in new productive ventures. It may be possible but it is unlikely, even by a circuitous route.

In some ways this discussion carries echoes of the events that led up to the Asian financial crisis of 1997. In the year before the crisis, international funds poured into the Asian emerging markets but in only a few countries did this extra portfolio investment lead to increased real investment in the domestic economy. On the contrary, it fed an upsurge in domestic credit and a burst of property speculation.

When the money washed out again this left many of the receiving countries in a hopeless mess. Some of them endured falls in output that rivalled what Germany and the United States had suffered during the 1930s. In the wake of the crisis, the stance taken by Malaysia to control capital inflows – which had previously been widely regarded as both antediluvian and deeply damaging – was now widely regarded as the appropriate way to deal with footloose international capital.

In view of this experience, and countless other episodes, why should we leave our exchange rate – and hence our international competitiveness – at the mercy of international capital holders? Of course, if they should some day fall out of love with UK assets then this would, other things equal, bring about the very drop in sterling that this pamphlet is advocating. But by the time that this happens huge damage may have been done to the UK's manufacturing and exporting businesses. Moreover, as and when international capital holders pull out, the change may be sudden and unpredictable, thereby causing serious problems in both the real economy and the financial system. (Arguably, this has already happened with the sharp fall of the pound induced by the Brexit vote.) It would surely be far better to discourage such inflows in the first place and thereby keep the exchange rate at a competitive and sustainable level.

Why the need for an exchange rate policy can easily be disparaged

1. Most British experience of exchange rate policy has involved trying to stop the pound from falling. This has inevitably led to crises as either the limited stock of international reserves has run low and/or interest rates have had to be increased, which is both unpopular and damaging to the domestic economy. By contrast, we are advocating a policy that can be used to reduce the pound and keep it low. This requires being prepared to build up international reserves and keeping interest rates low. Such a policy is much more readily sustainable and much more popular. There is no limit to the amount of your own currency that you can print to build up foreign currency reserves.

2. It is often argued that for the UK to adopt an exchange rate policy would be against our commitments to the G7. This is understandable. The obligations have been explicitly stated, as below:

Statement by G7 Finance Ministers and Central Bank Governors, February 12, 2013:
'We, the G7 Ministers and Governors, reaffirm our longstanding commitment to market determined exchange rates and to consult closely in regard to actions in foreign exchange markets. We reaffirm that our fiscal and monetary policies have been and will remain oriented towards meeting our respective domestic objectives using domestic instruments, and that we will not target exchange rates. We are agreed that excessive volatility and disorderly movements in exchange rates can have adverse implications for economic and financial stability. We will continue to consult closely on exchange markets and cooperate as appropriate.'

G20 Communique, November 15-16, 2015:
'We reaffirm our previous exchange rate commitments and will resist all forms of protectionism.'

Yet of the G7 grouping, three countries, namely Germany, France and Italy, are involved in a de facto policy of trying to depreciate the euro in an attempt to stimulate the eurozone economy. A fourth, Japan, is widely acknowledged to be doing the same through its policy of QE in pursuit of higher domestic inflation. Only the three Anglo-Saxon economies, the US, Canada and the UK, are left. Neither of the other two have significant current account problems in the way that the UK does.

3. Operating with a strong exchange rate is superficially very attractive for a government. In the short-term at least, it keeps inflation low, enriches consumers and seems to offer a vote of confidence from the markets in the government's policies. The latter can seem particularly valuable, and is well appreciated, when governments have a history of being plagued by currency weakness and fixed exchange rate crises. This is surely true of New Labour. The Labour Party had previously endured the gold standard crisis of 1931, the devaluation of 1949, and the devaluation of 1967. It had also witnessed the Conservative Party tearing itself apart after the ERM crisis of 1992. So, to have the exchange markets apparently approving of your policy/country, as they did in the years after 1997, was a source of great joy.

4. The language used to describe exchange rate movements makes it sound as though a high exchange rate is better. Not only do discussions contrast 'higher' with 'lower' but currencies are often described as 'strengthening' or 'weakening'. This language seems to suggest that a higher exchange rate is better.

5. The effects of exchange rate misalignments take time to come through. Companies do not withdraw from markets or dismantle plant – still less invest in new markets and new plant – at the drop of a hat. Accordingly, the sharp fluctuations in the UK's real exchange rate have meant that the response to even the periods of low exchange rates has been much weaker than it might otherwise have been.

6.   It is frequently argued by successful businesses that they can 'cope' with the current exchange rate. Such assertions are otiose. We know that they can cope. They are there. They are the survivors. But a suitable exchange rate policy has to cater also for the businesses that are no longer there – and even those that are as yet unborn. The objective of economic management should not be to ensure the highest average batting score but rather to ensure the highest score overall. This objective is not secured by deciding not to play your weakest six batsmen on the grounds that they are not as good as the others.

Conclusion

The case for action

The authors of this pamphlet are far from being enemies of market forces. On the contrary, both of us are supporters of the capitalist system and believe that, in general, market forces encourage people and institutions to behave in a way that maximises output and hence living standards.

But, especially in the realm of finance, markets can sometimes go awry. Moreover, market forces do not emerge from a vacuum. They are themselves a response to the economic conditions of the time and to the constellation of government and central bank policies, both here and abroad.

Exchange markets are particularly prone to misalignment with the economic fundamentals. In the wake of the collapse of the Bretton Woods system in 1971, many economists argued that the system's collapse created a brave new world in which market forces would push exchange rates to levels appropriate to the economic fundamentals.

These hopes were misplaced. The international monetary system is a mess and the misalignment of exchange rates and huge international payments imbalances have been a prime contributor (amongst others) to the world's recently poor economic growth. We hope that political leaders will again come to develop an international monetary system that deals with these problems and enables the world to reach its full potential. But you shouldn't hold your breath. In the meantime, the UK policy authorities have to fashion policy as best they can in the UK's interests, taking the world's monetary system as it is.

For most of the last 100 years the exchange rate has been at the centre of UK economic policy. For the last quarter century, however, it has been on the periphery. During this period, the UK's overseas trading performance has been poor, with the country running persistent current account deficits. The result has been a huge deterioration in the UK's international financial position. It has moved from being a substantial net creditor to being a substantial net debtor. This might not matter that much if the UK were also investing heavily at home. But it is not. Indeed, by international standards it is investing very little.

This situation has not developed as the result of a deliberate policy decision by UK governments. At no stage have the UK authorities deliberately set out to run down the UK's international assets or build up the UK's international liabilities. They have simply had no policy on this issue at all. Accordingly, what has happened to this important variable has simply been the passive response to other factors and policy decisions. The UK authorities have sleep-walked into a situation where the UK has sold many of its key assets to fund a short-term consumption binge and continues to grow more and more in hock to overseas asset holders. This situation has emerged as the incidental by-product of other policy decisions. The contribution of the UK authorities has simply been to ignore it.

The evidence is clear that the exchange rate for sterling has been too high. This has had major consequences for the whole UK economy and for its future. The strength of sterling has had three main sources:

(i)   The structure of UK macro policies which, unlike those in most of the rest of the world, takes no direct account of the exchange rate;

(ii)   Policies adopted in our main trading partner, the eurozone, deliberately to depreciate its currency, the euro;

(iii)   The attractions of UK assets to overseas wealth holders.

The UK cannot do anything directly to correct the second of these. But it can and should take action on the other two. We favour a two-pronged approach: a macro policy that accords a bigger role for the exchange rate; and a set of micro policies to diminish the attraction of UK assets to foreigners.

The point of having a more competitive currency would not be to take market share from rapidly developing countries, such as China or India, still less to seek to undermine their success. Admittedly, a lower pound would make UK exports more competitive against China and other emerging market countries, and thereby limit, deter, and even in some cases, reverse the leeching of manufacturing away from the UK. Nevertheless, the rise of the emerging markets has not been primarily due to the advantages of operating with an under-valued currency (although at times China has assuredly done so).

The really striking phenomenon, though, is the UK's loss of market share relative to other advanced countries. Here an over-valued exchange rate has played a definite role – and a competitive exchange rate could reverse much of the loss.

There is a view that if a low exchange rate is needed for the UK economy, then the markets will deliver it of their own accord. Yet this cannot be taken for granted – even after the sharp drop of the pound after the Brexit vote. We believe that, in the majority of cases, market forces do work – in the end. But the end can be a very long time in coming. In the meantime, the damage done to the economy by a severely misaligned exchange rate can be very severe. Indeed, the forces that are established by a misaligned exchange rate can be so serious that it may be impossible to return to the original growth path for decades subsequently.

Moreover, an exchange rate that is eventually driven by market forces to roughly the right level will not necessarily stay there. This is our profound worry after the Brexit vote has reduced the pound to a much more competitive level. Moreover, businesspeople involved in exporting and importing will not have the confidence that it will stay there. Accordingly, even if the exchange rate is established at a competitive level this may not have the full beneficial effect that it would do if the rate were believed in.

A policy of deliberately encouraging a competitive value for the currency is frequently inhibited by the authorities' fear that this may unleash a burst of inflation. In fact, in many cases those fears are unjustified. They would be unjustified now. The UK is in an era of ultra-low inflation and the Bank of England has evidently had difficulties in getting inflation up to its 2% target. It is hard to imagine a more propitious time for a successful depreciation of the currency.

After the Brexit vote produced a much lower exchange rate, many members of the commentariat fretted about the effects of the drop and discussed what the authorities might need to do to reverse it and 'stabilise the pound.' The right answer is: 'Nothing at all'. Indeed, the prime task now facing them is how to ensure that the pound stays at its new competitive level.

This is the latest – and most pressing – example that confirms the fundamental message of this pamphlet: the UK authorities need to put the exchange rate back where it belongs – at the centre of economic policy–making.